# ETERNAL VIGILANCE
## *The Story of*
### *Ida B. Wells-Barnett*

# ETERNAL VIGILANCE
## *The Story of*
## *Ida B. Wells-Barnett*

Greensboro, North Carolina

Eternal Vigilance:  The Story of Ida B. Wells-Barnett

Copyright © 2011 by Morgan Reynolds Publishing

Library of Congress Cataloging-in-Publication Data

Hinman, Bonnie.
 Eternal vigilance : the story of Ida B. Wells-Barnett / by Bonnie Hinman.
-- 1st ed.
     p. cm.
 Includes bibliographical references and index.
 ISBN 978-1-59935-111-7
1. Wells-Barnett, Ida B., 1862-1931--Juvenile literature. 2. African
American women civil rights workers--Biography--Juvenile literature. 3.
Civil rights workers--United States--Biography--Juvenile literature. 4.
African American women educators--Biography--Juvenile literature. 5.
African American women journalists--Biography--Juvenile literature. 6.
United States--Race relations--Juvenile literature. 7. African
Americans--Civil rights--History--Juvenile literature. 8. African
Americans--Social conditions--To 1964--Juvenile literature. 9.
Lynching--United States--History--Juvenile literature. I. Title.
 E185.97.W55H56 2010
 323.092--dc22
 [B]

                                    2010008144

Printed in the United States of America
First Edition

Book Cover and interior designed by:
Ed Morgan, navyblue design studio
Greensboro, NC

FOR MY GRANDSONS,
*Will, Parker, and Brody,*
*with the hope that they can grow up in a world*
*free from racial prejudice*

Ida B. Wells-Barnett

# TABLE OF CONTENTS

Cotton picking in Mississippi

# ONE

## A Slave's Daughter

On September 15, 1883, Ida B. Wells settled into a train seat for the short trip to her teaching job in Woodstock, Tennessee. Woodstock was only about ten miles from her home in Memphis, so she traveled back and forth on weekends.

Ida had purchased a newspaper and was deeply engrossed in her reading when the train's conductor, William Murray, came through the car collecting tickets. After looking at Ida's ticket, Murray told her he couldn't accept it. Ida took back the ticket without reply and went on reading.

After Murray had finished gathering tickets in the car, he came back to Ida. He told her she'd have to move, because she was seated in the ladies' car, which was reserved for whites. Ida had paid thirty cents for a first-class seat in the "colored car"—a section set aside for African Americans. But she had found a drunken white man seated there, along with swirls of smoke, so moved to the first-class ladies' car, believing it was her right to do so.

Again, Murray asked Ida to move. She refused. Then, "he tried to drag me out of my seat," Ida recalled. Murray even ripped the sleeve off of her dress, as he tried to pry her from the seat. But Ida was determined not be moved: "The moment he caught hold of my arm I fastened my teeth in the back of his hand."

Ida and the conductor scuffled as the other passengers rose to watch. Ida gained the advantage when she braced her feet on the seat in front of her and held onto the back of that seat. The conductor yanked at her but was a bit leery of the young woman who had already given him a nasty bite.

At last, Murray asked the white passengers to help him, and together they managed to drag Ida out of her seat and down the aisle.

Of the men's actions, Ida wrote, "They were encouraged to do this by the attitude of the white ladies and gentlemen in the car; some of them even stood on the seats so that they could get a good view and continued applauding the conductor for his brave stand."

Ida decided to get off the train rather than be forced to sit where swearing, drinking, and smoking were often overlooked by the conductor. Ida's clothing had a few tears and she herself had some bruises, but it was her sense of justice that suffered the most damage.

Ida B. Wells was born during the Civil War on July 16, 1862. In less than six months, Abraham Lincoln would sign the Emancipation Proclamation, freeing the slaves in all states that were in rebellion against the Union. Ida's parents, James and Elizabeth Wells, were slaves, which made Ida a slave, too.

James Wells was the son of a white plantation owner, Morgan Wells, and one of Wells's slaves, named Peggy. Morgan Wells had no children with his white wife, Polly, and treated James with much affection. James experienced very little of the cruel treatment often given slaves on a cotton plantation.

When James turned eighteen, Morgan Wells took him to Holly Springs, Mississippi, to be apprenticed to Spires Bolling, a well-to-do builder who planned to teach James carpentry. It was expected that James would return to the plantation with a valuable skill.

Ida as a young woman

Ida's mother, Elizabeth Warrenton, had been born in Virginia. She hadn't escaped the beatings, the auction block, being separated from her family, and all the other miseries of slave life. She worked for the Bolling family as a cook.

During James's apprenticeship, his father died unexpectedly, and just as unexpectedly came the Civil War. In spite of the uproar of war, love bloomed between James and Elizabeth. Slaves were not allowed to marry legally then, but many joined their lives in a less formal way, as did James and Elizabeth.

Soon Ida was born, and a few months later Emancipation was announced. Holly Springs was in the path of both North and South armies, and both forces traded the town back and forth several times. One of the most spectacular trades happened in December 1862, when Ida was five months old.

Union General Ulysses S. Grant was in control of Holly Springs and had established a huge supply base there. Convinced of the security of Holly Springs, Grant took the bulk of his forces south through Mississippi. A Confederate cavalry brigade surprised the occupying forces and captured the entire town of Holly Springs and all the supplies in it.

What the Confederate troops couldn't take with them, they burned in a spectacular fire complete with exploding ammunition. Union troops took the town back the next day, but the damage had been done. Grant was forced to pillage the countryside in order to supply his army.

After Emancipation, James and Elizabeth legalized their marriage and stayed on to work for Bolling, living in a small tenant house that Bolling owned. By now, James was a skilled carpenter and was valuable to his employer. He earned a decent salary and provided an adequate living for his growing family.

James and Elizabeth faced a big change after James went to vote for the first time. This was probably late in 1867 after Mississippi black men had been given the right to vote. African Americans usually favored the Republicans, the political party of Abraham Lincoln. White landowners were overwhelmingly Democrats and often tried to influence their former slaves to vote for the Democratic candidates.

Bolling did this to James. He told James that if he didn't vote Democrat, he'd lose his job. James refused to be intimidated and voted Republican. When he came home, he found that he had been locked out of the shop where he worked for Bolling.

James didn't raise a fuss or even try to change Bolling's mind. He just walked to the local stores, bought his own tools, and moved his family out of the Bolling tenant house. By the time Bolling realized what had happened, the Wells family was gone. They moved into a house that James rented.

James was able to find work on his own because of his excellent reputation as a carpenter and his hardworking ways. The Wells's family life went on as before.

Ida's childhood was very different from that of her parents. "Our job," Ida recalled, "was to go to school and learn all we could." James and Elizabeth were adamant that their children get the education that they had been denied as slaves. Ida said she couldn't remember when she started school because she was so young. But she did remember that her mother went to school with her children until she learned to read well enough to read the Bible.

The Wells's attitude about education was common for blacks after the Civil War. Freed slaves saw education as one of the keys to making new lives for themselves. Most slaves had been forbidden to learn to read or write. They flooded the schools that were started during and after the war.

A family on a cotton patch near Vicksburg, Mississippi

In 1865, the U.S. Congress established the Freedmen's Bureau, a federal agency formed to help freed slaves. The bureau provided many services for freed slaves in the South, but its greatest successes came when it started schools for freed black men, women, and their children. It was common for missionary societies from the northern states to work with the Freedmen's Bureau and send teachers to the new schools.

The Freedmen's Bureau, along with the Methodist Episcopal Church, founded and ran the school that Ida and her brothers and sisters attended. Originally called Shaw University and later renamed Rust College, the school educated black students from elementary age up through a four-year high school level program.

Ida's school first met in Asbury Methodist Church but eventually had its own building. Ida was an excellent student who loved to read. As the oldest of a family that would eventually have eight children, Ida had many chores, but school came first.

Elizabeth Wells, who was deeply religious, took her children to Sunday school every week. One of Ida's weekly chores was to get her siblings bathed on Saturday night and prepare their clothes for Sunday morning.

Elizabeth sometimes told her children about her slave days and how she had been beaten and sold away from her family. Her experiences were common among former slaves. After the war, many freed slaves roamed the South searching for lost relatives. They looked for wives, husbands, children, and parents who had been left behind or sold away from their families.

James Wells had less to say about his youth as a slave. But annual visits from his mother, Peggy, sometimes gave Ida glimpses of that life. Peggy had married after the war and lived with her husband on a farm, where they tilled many acres of land and raised pigs.

Ida remembered one visit when her grandmother and father talked about the old days. Peggy told her son that Morgan Wells's wife wanted to see James and his children.

"Mother," James said, "I never want to see that old woman as long as I live. I'll never forget how she had you stripped and whipped the day after the old man died, and I am never going to see her."

The old man James referred to was his white father, the plantation owner. "I guess it is all right for you to take care of her and forgive her for what she did to you," James said, "but she could have starved to death if I'd had my say-so. She certainly would have, if it hadn't been

The KKK began as a social club started by
Confederate soldiers but quickly became a hate group.

for you." Ida didn't understand this story when she first heard it as a child, but she later came to see it as a window into her father's feelings about slavery.

James Wells felt strongly about many issues and often attended political meetings. One of the most prominent political groups was the Loyal League, a Republican organization created to protect black voting rights. This organization was active throughout the South. The Loyal League had been founded by white Republicans across the South and was often controlled by them.

The Ku Klux Klan was active at this time, as well. Some former Confederate soldiers had started the KKK in 1866 as a social club in Tennessee. Within a year, it turned into a hate group dedicated to harassing and murdering African Americans. Klan members did their dirty work at night as they rode on horses through the countryside. They rode to homes with torches blazing and threatened the black occupants within. Often they claimed to simply be reminding the blacks of their proper place by intimidating them into subservience to whites. Klansmen wore flowing white robes complete with hoods and tall, pointed hats. They intended to keep their identities secret, but many were well known in their communities. If an African American man had been accused of a crime, the Klan might burn his home or even murder him as punishment for the alleged crime.

One of Ida's first memories was of reading the newspaper to her father and his friends. She remembered hearing them talk about the Klan at these gatherings. She didn't know what they were talking about but later said, "I knew dimly that it meant something fearful, by the anxious way my mother walked the floor at night when my father was out to a political meeting."

In spite of the political turmoil in Mississippi and the whole South at that time, Ida's childhood was a relatively secure one. Her parents earned a steady income and provided a home as well as support for their children to get an education. The future looked bright for sixteen-year-old Ida as she traveled to visit her grandmother Peggy on the farm in late summer 1878. But Ida's carefree childhood would soon end.

# TWO

## *Teacher Ida*

Ida had taken the train to visit her grandmother before. She worked on the farm during these visits, but it was a break from her many duties with her brothers and sisters. During that summer of 1878, a yellow fever epidemic was sweeping through the Mississippi River Valley area.

Yellow fever is spread by mosquitoes, but people of Ida's time didn't know that. They thought that the fever was spread by swamp vapors. In reality, it was the mosquitoes in the swampy areas that were responsible.

Because Holly Springs was on high ground, town officials assumed that yellow fever wouldn't affect their town. They allowed residents of Memphis and other towns to come to Holly Springs. In an ordinary year, everyone might have escaped the fever, but 1878's strain was particularly deadly and widespread. It had been a damp summer, and mosquitoes were everywhere.

The fever soon struck Holly Springs residents in huge numbers, and many died. If families could flee the town, they did. When Ida heard about the epidemic, she assumed that her family had left home and traveled to her Aunt Belle's home in the countryside near Holly

Springs to stay until the danger had passed. No letters arrived, but she thought that mail service had been stopped.

One day in September, three men arrived on horseback at the farm. Ida recognized them as friends of her parents. She thought they had come to visit and bring news.

The men handed Ida a letter, which she read: "Jim and Lizzie Wells have both died of the fever. They died within 24 hours of each other. The children are all at home and the Howard Association has put a woman there to take care of them. Send word to Ida."

Ida reeled with shock. Her only thought now was to get to her brothers and sisters. At first, her grandmother Peggy didn't want her to go back to Holly Springs, where the epidemic still raged. But finally a letter arrived from the doctor in charge saying that Ida should come. Only then was Ida allowed to board a train for home.

Ida discovered that all the children had contracted the fever except for Eugenia, Ida's oldest sister. Two of the children were still ill but recovering. Sadly, she discovered that her nine-month-old brother, Stanley, had died. They all wanted to know why she had dared come back to town, but they seemed relieved to see her. Nurses from the Howard Association had been caring for the children, but they would leave town when the epidemic subsided. The Howard Association was a benevolent organization that was founded after a yellow fever epidemic in 1855. A forerunner of the Red Cross, it sent doctors and nurses to stricken areas.

Eugenia told Ida all that had happened during the epidemic. Their father had helped nurse stricken townspeople and built coffins for the dead. He returned home each day only long enough to bring food and check on his family. Elizabeth came down with the fever first. James hurried home to nurse her but soon became ill, too. He died the day before his wife did.

Eugenia said that a kindly Dr. D. H. Gray, who had been sent by the Howard Association, watched over the family. He sent nurses to care for the family and locked up their savings when Elizabeth saw a nurse going through James Wells's pockets. Dr. Gray returned their money. He told Ida how her father had comforted and prayed with the fever victims, who lay in a courthouse that had been converted to a hospital.

The epidemic wound down by the end of October. The Wells family was healthy again, but it wasn't clear what would happen to them next. What was very clear was that Ida's childhood was finished.

As soon as the epidemic was over, a meeting was held at the Wells house to decide the fate of the children. James Wells had belonged to the Masons, which was a men's fraternal society. It was a club with secret rituals that was very popular in the late nineteenth century. Masons were community minded and considered it their duty to help the families of their members no matter what the need. At the end of a long discussion, it was decided that the two little girls—Annie, age five, and Lily, age two—would go live with two different families. The boys—James, eleven, and George, nine—would be adopted by men who hoped that they had inherited their father's carpentry abilities.

The Masons are a fraternal order to which Ida's father belonged.

This left only Eugenia and Ida. Ida was considered old enough to be on her own. Eugenia was a different story. She was partially paralyzed by a crippling disorder that had twisted her spine. Scoliosis had hit Eugenia two years earlier when she was about twelve. She couldn't walk and would always need special care. The Masons decided that Eugenia would have to be sent to the poorhouse, a public facility for the old and crippled who didn't have family to care for them.

Ida listened quietly while the discussion proceeded. Then, she later wrote, "When all this had been arranged to their satisfaction, I, who said nothing before and had not even been consulted, calmly announced that they were not going to take any of the children anywhere; I said that it would make my father and mother turn over in their graves to know their children had been scattered like that and that we owned the house and if the Masons would help me find work, I would take care of them."

The Masons protested at first, but Ida thought they were a little relieved not to have to worry over the problem. Two of the men, Bob Miller and James Hall, were appointed as guardians. They advised Ida to take the examination to become a country school teacher.

Ida had been in school at Shaw University (by then informally called Rust College) in Holly Springs when her parents died, but she hadn't been taking the teacher training program of study. However, teachers were so much in demand that a student could become one by passing a test that determined if he or she was qualified. Because of her youth and inexperience, Ida would become a country schoolteacher first. That test was easier than the one given to prospective teachers for city schools. Later, she would study for and pass that test, too.

Because her parents had been hardworking and careful with their money, Ida was able to take a few months to pass her test and otherwise prepare for her new career. Their home was paid for, and there was at

A 1861 panoramic map looking south from
Vienna, Illinois, to Holly Springs, Mississippi

least three hundred dollars in savings to support the Wells children until Ida could begin earning.

However, problems arose even before Ida could begin her new job. Rumors flew that Ida was having an affair with a white man and needed the Wells house as a secret meeting place. Ida was astounded to find that anyone could even think such a thing of her. She had been sheltered by her parents and had never even been allowed to be among men or boys without supervision. The rumors were very upsetting to Ida. Soon, her grandmother Peggy came to live with the family to try to put a stop to the talk. Peggy was in her seventies, but to help out with expenses she worked during the day while the children were in school. The hard work took its toll, and Peggy collapsed from a stroke. Peggy's daughter came from the country to take her mother back to the farm, where she died a few years later.

By the time Ida was ready to start her new job, a friend of Elizabeth's had agreed to stay with the children during the week. The country school was six miles away from Holly Springs, so Ida stayed at the school or in the homes of her students. On Friday afternoons, Ida climbed aboard a big mule and rode home to spend the weekends with her siblings. There was no rest for Ida, however, as she spent the whole time washing, ironing, cleaning, and cooking for the family.

It was a punishing routine for young Ida. Teaching turned out to be harder than she expected. There were too many pupils and not enough books and supplies. Many of the students were as old as or older than Ida, making discipline a problem. These problems were common in the South in the years following Reconstruction.

Reconstruction officially began in March 1867 when Congress passed the Reconstruction Act over President Andrew Johnson's veto. This act along with the one that had established the Freedman's Bureau attempted to provide a measure of protection and opportunity for the freed slaves of the South. In the two years since the Civil War had ended in April 1865, conditions for southern blacks had steadily deteriorated. It seemed that white Southerners were working toward a new kind of slavery for their former slaves. African Americans were taken advantage of in almost every way possible as they struggled to find work and homes for their families. Most freed slaves were illiterate, which led to unfair contracts for labor and tenant farming. Former slaves moved from their previous homes on cotton plantations to the cities, but they found few good jobs there.

The Reconstruction Act divided the South into five military districts, with federal troops stationed in each to enforce the new laws that protected black citizens. Within a year, blacks were being elected to political office after being allowed to vote for the first time. With the Freedmen Bureau's help, conditions improved, and black citizens began making real economic and political progress.

Political disagreement between Republicans and Democrats led to continuing arguments over Reconstruction policies. Radical Republicans were the most adamant about giving freed slaves every possible opportunity, while southern Democrats wanted to preserve states' rights, particularly those of the former Confederate states. Moderate Republicans tried to take a middle course.

Meanwhile, white supremacists in the southern states were doing everything they could to terrorize blacks into not voting.

Reconstruction limped along until the presidential election of 1876, when it fell apart altogether. Republican Rutherford B. Hayes ran against Democrat Samuel J. Tilden. The election came under dispute when Tilden had 184 electoral votes and needed 185 to win. Hayes had 165 votes. Twenty votes were disputed. After months of negotiating, a compromise was agreed to. Hayes would be president, but he would agree to withdraw federal troops from the South, ending Reconstruction.

President Rutherford B. Hayes

Ida lived through Reconstruction and the difficult years that followed. She saw firsthand the complicated process that tried to bring black Americans freedom and often failed. Her little country school was a perfect example of the difficulties. Schools were segregated, with black schools given less of everything than the white schools.

Ida persevered and found bright spots in her hardworking days. She read in the evenings when she was staying at her school. Reading was her chief pleasure and enabled her to educate herself. Apparently, Ida also attended classes at Rust College during her summer vacations. This period of her life isn't well documented, but it seems that some kind of problem at Rust forced her to quit attending classes there. She later referred to that time as "my darkest days."

Ida had a fiery temper and likely tangled with the president of Rust, W. W. Hooper. She never explained what happened but did express regret years later in her diary. She described her "tempestuous, rebellious, hard headed willfulness" during that period of her life. She also wrote that she no longer blamed Professor Hooper for cutting short her scholastic career but rather blamed herself.

Finally, Ida got some relief from her demanding life when her Aunt Belle offered for the two boys and Eugenia to come to the farm and live there. Eventually, the boys would be apprenticed as carpenters, and Aunt Belle promised to care for Eugenia.

Another aunt, Fannie, was widowed and lived in Memphis with her three young children. She invited Ida and the two little girls to live with her.

These two aunts' offers must have seemed like gifts from heaven to the burdened Ida. The moves were arranged, and Ida found a teaching job at a country school about ten miles from Memphis. This time she rode the train instead of her mule when she came home for weekend visits. And, it was during this time that Ida encountered William Murray, the conductor who wanted her to move from the first-class ladies' section of the train.

Increasingly in the early 1880s, African Americans were expected to keep away from whites in public places. The federal Civil Rights Act

The federal Civil Rights Act of 1875 attempted to eliminate
segregation in public places such as the train station pictured here,
but southern states still allowed separate areas for whites and blacks.

of 1875 had attempted to eliminate any segregation in public places, but southern states soon passed their own legislation to alter or negate the federal law.

After the scuffle with Murray, Ida returned to Memphis determined to file a lawsuit against the Chesapeake & Ohio Railroad. She marched into the office of the only African American lawyer in Memphis and hired him to file a discrimination suit against the railroad. Thomas F. Cassells filed the suit, but after many delays, Ida became convinced that he had been "bought off by the [rail] road." She fired him and hired a white lawyer, James M. Greer.

Greer did a good job; Ida won her case and was awarded damages. While this suit was still going on, Ida was escorted out of a train car for a second time. She promptly filed another lawsuit. This suit was also decided in her favor, and the court awarded her five hundred dollars in damages in late 1884. Ida wrote: "I can see to this day the headlines in the *Memphis Appeal* announcing DARKY DAMSEL GETS DAMAGES."

Ida's faith in the court system that had agreed with her was broken three years later when the Tennessee Supreme Court overturned the lower court's decision on appeal. The Supreme Court asserted that the railroad had indeed provided equal accommodations for African Americans in a separate car. This was arguably not true, as the smoky second-class car could hardly have been considered equal accommodations. The court further stated that Ida was trying to harass the railroad with her suit.

Ida was bitterly disappointed about the unexpected loss and expressed her feelings in her diary. "I felt so disappointed," she wrote, "because I had hoped such great things from my suit for my people generally. I have firmly believed all along that the law was on our side and would, when we appealed to it, give us justice. I feel shorn of that belief and utterly discouraged, and just now if it were possible would gather my race in my arms and fly far away with them."

Other than the train incidents, Ida's life was busy but largely uneventful. The country school where she taught was undersupplied, and Ida often felt that she was not properly trained to be a teacher. She attempted to remedy this lack by reading widely from the works of Shakespeare, Dickens, Louisa May Alcott, and others and by attending special summer classes for teachers. These were called teachers' institutes and were offered by Memphis colleges such as Fisk and LeMoyne.

Perhaps most revealing about Ida's determination and persistence was her later confession of her true feelings about teaching. "I never cared for teaching," she wrote, "but I had always been very conscientious in trying to do my work honestly. There seemed nothing else to do for a living except menial work, and I could not have made a living at that."

Ida commuted to her job, attended church, and often taught Sunday school. But her quiet life ended rather abruptly in the fall of 1884. Aunt Fannie decided to move to California and take Annie and Lily with her. Since the boys and Eugenia remained on the farm, this left Ida by herself for the first time in her life.

This freedom was both exciting and a bit frightening for twenty-two-year-old Ida. Memphis in the 1880s had an African American elite class that had developed after the Civil War. Ida's position as a schoolteacher offered her entrance into that class. She joined a lyceum that met on Friday evenings each week. A lyceum is an educational club that sponsors literary, musical, and other programs. Ida's fellow club members were mostly public school teachers. They took turns presenting essays, recitations, and debates. Their lyceum also had a literary journal called the *Evening Star*, which was produced by one of the members.

*Ida read works by Louisa May Alcott to further her education.*

Through the lyceum, Ida met members of the black elite, and soon she was involved in a whirl of social and cultural activities. She attended parties, the theater, and concerts, and she took excursions and short trips.

Ida loved the activity, but there was a downside. Although she was now making more money (sixty dollars a month), she did not make enough to support her many activities and provide funds to send to Aunt Fannie for Lily and Annie. She lived in a series of rooming houses, which were plentiful and relatively cheap, but her new social position made many demands on her purse.

Social events required fashionable clothing and accessories. A popular custom of the time was to exchange photographs among friends, so that required Ida to take new photos rather frequently.

The result was that Ida was often short of money. Her diary entries during her Memphis years detailed some of her struggles. In her first diary entry on December 29, 1885, she wrote of her money problems: "Looking back at my debts I am thankful I could not accomplish my purpose and borrow money to get away—I would have been more deeply in debt and I am very sorry I did not resist the impulse to buy that cloak; I would have been $15.00 richer."

During this social whirl, Ida ventured into journalism. She wrote about her experiences with the railroad lawsuit for a local weekly newspaper for blacks called the *Living Way*. R. N. Countee, a local Baptist pastor, published the paper and distributed most of the copies to his congregation. Reverend Countee probably heard of Ida through the lyceum and asked her to write about her experiences. He liked what she wrote and asked her to submit more articles and essays for his paper. Countee couldn't afford to pay her but promised that she could write about serious issues.

Ida could scarcely believe her good fortune. She enjoyed writing and found that she had opinions on many subjects. Countee's invitation opened the door to a new life for Ida.

# THREE

## *A New Calling*

Ida had chosen the pen name "Iola," and under that byline she continued to write for the *Living Way*. Black-run newspapers of that time often commented on or reprinted each other's articles, so her essays gained a wide readership. The *New York Globe* first commented on Ida's *Living Way* articles about the railroad suit in May 1884. The *Globe*, later called the *Freeman* and finally the *Age*, was edited by T. Thomas Fortune. Fortune's paper had subscribers across the country, so Ida soon had an interested audience beyond Reverend Countee's Baptist church congregation.

In January 1885, the *Freeman* ran an article written by Ida about the lawsuit. Several of Ida's articles were reprinted that year in the *Freeman*, including ones on southern editors and black leadership. By 1886, Ida was contributing letters and articles to such publications as the Kansas City *Gate City Press* and the *Little Rock Sun*. Payment, if offered at all, was usually in copies (which Ida could sell) or subscriptions. Even as Ida began to think of herself as a journalist, it was unrealistic for her to think that she could make a living from her writing.

Other black women journalists worked in the U.S. at that time, but most of them wrote only about family issues. Ida didn't scorn writing about and for women. She wrote often about home and family and education. One of her convictions was that ordinary men and women (uneducated beyond basics) needed guidance to improve themselves. However, she had no intention of limiting her guidance to family or education problems.

Ida wrote constantly about racial issues. She deplored the increasing segregation of black Americans and was as likely to criticize blacks for not fighting against it as she was to criticize whites for being bigots. She complained that prominent black citizens did little to help the downtrodden members of their own race. Ida had opinions about everything, and most people had equally strong positive or negative opinions about her. It was hard to stay neutral when it came to the fiery Ida.

Ida continued to teach during the day while writing at night and on weekends. Her lukewarm attitude toward teaching hadn't improved, but the newspaper writing gave her a rewarding outlet. Conditions in the black schools of Memphis were much better than in many other southern cities, but Ida still had as many as seventy students at a time in her classes. Discipline was difficult if not impossible, and Ida often wondered if she was teaching her students anything at all.

In the summer of 1886, Ida made plans to go to a teacher's convention in Topeka, Kansas. She would travel with teacher friends by train, taking advantage of a special reduced-fare group tour rate. These special tours were popular in the late 1800s and were known as excursions. Before she could depart, she received a letter from Aunt Fannie in Visalia, California. Aunt Fannie wanted Ida to come to Visalia and apply for a teaching position there.

Ida was afraid that Aunt Fannie was going to tell her that she could no longer care for Lily and Annie, who were ten and thirteen. Ida did not want to leave Memphis but felt she owed Aunt Fannie a huge debt. In the end, she wrote to Fannie to inform her that she would visit for the summer but not settle there. Ida booked a further excursion from

Topeka to California and arrived there on August 1 after attending the conference in Topeka.

The sisters were thrilled to see each other, but Ida was sorry to see that her aunt looked old beyond her years. This discovery triggered a surge of guilt for Ida, as she assumed that her aunt's weary face was the result of caring for the two extra children. Ida's stay in Visalia quickly became a struggle, as Aunt Fannie tried to convince her to stay and teach at the black school there. Ida couldn't make up her mind what to do. She wanted to return to Memphis but felt her duty required her to stay in Visalia or take her sisters back to Memphis.

She didn't have the money for the girls' train fares, but she wrote to a Memphis businessman, Robert Church, to see if he could loan her $150. He was known as a philanthropist, so Ida was hopeful he would agree. But as the days of August ticked by, she didn't hear from Church. At last, she decided to accept her fate and teach in Visalia.

Visalia was a small town south of Fresno, California. Ida could see that there was little social or cultural life there. Her aunt was satisfied because Ida was able to find work, but Ida saw Visalia as a prison. It was as segregated as any small southern town of that time. The white school was a handsome building. The black children were sent to a rundown school, where they barely had any books or equipment.

When school started, Ida found teaching in Visalia to be just as uninspiring as she had feared it

Robert Church

would be. Rescue arrived in a telegram on the second day of school. Some new friends Ida had met at the education convention in Topeka wired her to say that they had arranged a teaching job for her in Kansas City. Then two days later, she received Church's reply to her request to borrow money. He enclosed the money and assured Ida that her teaching position was still open in Memphis if she wanted to return.

Ida quickly decided to accept the Kansas City position and prepared for her two sisters to go there. Her older sister, Annie, begged to be left behind because she didn't want to be separated from her cousin. In the end, Aunt Fannie seemed eager that Annie be allowed to stay with her cousin. That left Ida and Lily to travel to Kansas City.

When Ida reached Kansas City, she discovered that she had replaced a less-experienced teacher who had been employed for the position. The school officials, eager to get experienced teachers, had withdrawn their job offer to the younger woman when Ida agreed to teach for them. Ida soon found that the teachers in her new school resented her for taking the other woman's job. She finished her first day but went straight to the principal's office to submit her resignation.

Ida and Lily packed up again and headed for Memphis, where Ida arrived in time to start the first day of school. The sisters settled in at their boarding house for another school year. Ida was clearly pleased to be back in Memphis. She later said of her departure from Kansas City, "I breathed freer after it was all over and I turned my face to the only home I know."

Ida continued to write, and a new journalism opportunity presented itself in October 1886. The editor of the lyceum paper, the *Evening Star*, left her position, and Ida was invited to take over the job. Ida enjoyed writing and editing the paper and gained name recognition for her other more serious articles and essays. Her work for the *Living Way* continued to be reprinted widely in other black newspapers.

In late 1886, she first received monetary payment for her writing when William J. Simmons, editor of the *American Baptist*, offered to pay her one dollar a week to write for his publication. Ida described this exciting event in her autobiography: "He wanted me as a correspondent of his paper and offered me the lavish sum of one dollar a letter weekly! It was the first time anyone had offered to pay me for the work I had enjoyed doing. I had never dreamed of receiving any pay, for I had been too happy over the thought that the papers were giving me space."

Wells considered Simmons her mentor in journalism. "In every way he could Dr. Simmons encouraged me to be a newspaper woman, and whatever fame I achieved in that line I owe in large measure to his influence and encouragement." Simmons also offered to pay her way to the National Colored Press Association Convention in 1887 if she would contract to write a certain number of articles for his publication.

Ida's journalistic output up through 1887 was huge considering that she still taught school during the week, maintained her social life, and attended church and cultural activities frequently. She even planned to write a novel with a friend. Although she did eventually have a short story published, the novel project never materialized.

The National Colored Press Association Convention, held in late summer 1887 in Louisville, Kentucky, was a high point of Ida's early writing career. Simmons made good on his promise to pay her way to the convention in return for her regular articles. "I went to Louisville to the first press convention I had ever attended," Ida said later, "and was tickled pink over the attention I received from those veterans of the press."

Apparently, the 1887 convention was the first to invite women delegates. Three women journalists were there, but Ida attracted the most attention. She delivered a paper on newspaper editing and spoke about women journalists' roles at a banquet. The convention was held yearly so that editors could exchange ideas and make valuable connections. Ida made a positive impression on the attendees and was elected to office in the organization within two years.

Ida enjoyed attending conventions and conferences. She traveled to teacher and church meetings and to political gatherings all over the country. In July 1888, she went to Indianapolis, Indiana, to attend a meeting between black Democrats and independents.

Since most African Americans were still Republicans, this meeting was controversial. It turned out to be heated as well, as the attendees argued over political appointments.

It was at this conference that Ida met T. Thomas Fortune in person. Ida had earlier reported being under-impressed with his physical likeness when she first saw his picture. She had written in her Memphis diary, "With his long hair, curling about his forehead and his spectacles he looks more like the dude of the period than the strong, sensible, brainy man I have pictured."

Ida didn't record how she felt about Fortune after she met him in person at the conference, but Fortune wrote of Ida: "If Iola were a man, she would be a humming independent in politics. She has plenty of nerve, and is as sharp as a steel trap, and she has no sympathy for humbug." Fortune would prove to be a strong ally for Ida.

In 1888, a new newspaper started in Memphis. The *Free Speech* was edited by Reverend Taylor Nightingale and headquartered in his church, Beale Street Baptist. Soon after he started the paper, he merged it with the *Marion Headlight*, which was edited by J. L. Fleming and had previously been quartered near Memphis in Marion, Arkansas. Fleming had been run out of Marion by whites who lived there. Nightingale and Fleming joined their two papers and called it the *Free Speech and Headlight*.

Ida had written for the Marion paper and soon was asked to write for the new *Free Speech and Headlight*. She negotiated a deal with the two owners to sell her a one-third interest in the newspaper. By summer 1889, Ida had saved enough money to purchase her share in the paper. She thus became one of the country's first female black newspaper editors and owners. She took over most of the editing while Fleming served as business manager and Reverend Nightingale as sales manager. Nightingale's congregation each Sunday accounted for a good portion of their sales.

Ida dived into her new job with enthusiasm and a sharp journalistic pen. Newspapers often disagreed strongly with each other, particularly about political issues. They commonly printed condemnations

T. Thomas Fortune

of each other's viewpoints. Ida didn't escape this warfare and entered the fray when she thought it necessary. One difference for her was that her critics blasted her for being a woman as often as they criticized her political views. Ida was sensitive to this kind of criticism but occasionally used her gender to further her career. She was sometimes called "Princess of the Press," a nickname that reflected her gender along with her journalistic skills. Far from being offended at this title, Ida took it as a compliment. A female journalist was rare, and a black one rarer still. Ida used this fact to promote her own career and the issues she addressed.

In 1889, Ida attended the National Colored Press Association Convention in Washington, D.C., where she was elected secretary to the organization. That convention was filled with excitement for Ida, as she met Frederick Douglass for the first time.

Douglass was the most famous of African Americans at that time. A former slave, he had campaigned against slavery before the Civil War. In spite of danger to himself, he had given speeches and written widely about the evils of slavery. He was instrumental in gaining European support for abolition. In 1889, his was still a strong voice for black rights. Douglass was pleased with the determination he saw in the young Ida Wells and served as a mentor to her until his death in 1895.

In these early years, Ida condemned white discrimination against blacks but also criticized blacks who, by their failure to speak up, seemed to offer support for segregation. One of the bigger issues that arose was the new Mississippi state constitution.

In 1890, Mississippi held a constitutional convention to update and improve the state document. The resulting constitution provided ways to keep blacks from voting. The Fifteenth Amendment to the U.S. Constitution had been ratified in 1870. It instructed states that they could not deny the right to vote to people on the basis of race, color, or previous condition of servitude. Mississippi neatly sidestepped the issue by instituting poll taxes—which required voters to pay a tax before voting—and allowing a literacy test to be administered to prospective voters.

Black voting in the South had been discouraged in many ways since Reconstruction ended, but Mississippi was the first state to write the exclusions into its constitution. Discrimination had usually been done on a local level. It included confusing ballot box systems, poll taxes, no voting places in black areas, and a requirement that a prospective voter demonstrate his understanding of the U.S. Constitution. Technically, these methods applied to whites, too, but enforcement was selective.

The *Free Speech* (the paper's name had been shortened after Ida took over), under Ida's editorship, expressed great outrage at Mississippi's efforts to officially stop blacks from voting. Ida's sharpest barbs were directed at Isaiah Montgomery, who as the only black delegate to the Mississippi convention, had voted in favor of the new constitution. Montgomery was a successful landowner and prominent politician.

A 1870 lithograph commemorating the celebration in
Baltimore of the enactment of the Fifteenth Amendment

Isaiah Montgomery was a successful
landowner and prominent politician.

Ida and other African Americans were appalled that Montgomery had voted in favor of the flawed constitution. Ida's strong criticism in the *Free Speech* prompted Montgomery to visit Ida in order to explain his vote. Of this visit, Ida later stated, "Mr. Montgomery came to Memphis to explain, but although we never agreed that his course had been the right one, we became the best of friends, and he helped to increase the circulation of the paper wonderfully by sending me all through the Delta."

Ida's trip through the Delta took place in the summer of 1891. Montgomery's invitation smoothed her way as she traveled throughout the Mississippi River Delta gathering news and signing up new subscribers for the *Free Speech*. The increased business for the newspaper became particularly important in fall 1891, when Ida lost her teaching job.

Ida had written an article for the *Free Speech* that was critical of black schools in Memphis. She condemned not only the conditions in the buildings but also the training and character of some of the younger teachers. She wrote, "It had been charged that some of these teachers had little to recommend them save an illicit friendship with members of the school board." She asked Reverend Nightingale to sign the article as his, but he refused. She knew that such statements might get her fired, but she proceeded anyhow, feeling that schoolchildren were suffering from having unqualified teachers.

In spite of the uproar created by her article, Ida wasn't fired immediately. At least one other paper agreed with her. But when fall came, Ida's name wasn't on the list of teachers whose contracts had been renewed. Notification came too late for Ida to get another position.

Ida's lawyer asked for an explanation from the school board as to why Ida's contract hadn't been renewed. School board officials replied that they declined to employ a teacher who was so critical of them. Ida wrote of her dismissal, "Of course I had rather feared that might be the result; but I had taken a chance in the interest of the children of our race and had lost out." She was disappointed, however, that the parents she talked to did not appreciate what she had tried to do for their children. They thought she was wrong to do something that could lead to losing her job.

She wrote later of the lesson she learned from this experience: "But I thought it was right to strike a blow against a glaring evil and I did not regret it. Up to that time I had felt that any fight made in the interest of the race would have its support. I learned then that I could not count on that."

Ida immediately launched into expanding the paper's circulation in order to increase her share enough to offset the loss of her teacher's income. She had already made her summer tour of the Delta and soon undertook other trips to drum up new subscribers. She succeeded, and soon upped her income to within ten dollars of what she had received monthly from teaching. Ida also had more time to work in organizations such as the Southern Afro-American Press Association and the National Afro-American League. Neither organization lasted for long, but their formation paved the way for later successful organizations.

Overall, Ida was quite happy with her new career as a journalist. But in March 1892, events in Memphis changed her life drastically and set her on the path to a new destiny.

# FOUR
## *Lynching at the Curve*

In Memphis, there was an area called the "Curve" because of the sharp curve the streetcar line made there. Both African Americans and whites lived in the neighborhood, but black residents predominated. The area had been served by a white-owned grocery store for some time. Store owner W. H. Barrett had a monopoly on the business in the neighborhood and wanted to keep it that way.

In 1889, some black residents had combined their savings and started another grocery store, which they called the People's Grocery Company. Thomas Moss, a postal carrier and good friend of Ida's, had invested in the store and served as the president of the corporation. He continued to work as a mailman while his co-investors, Calvin McDowell and Will Stewart, ran the grocery store during the day. Moss helped out on evenings and weekends. As they began to take away some of Barrett's customers, bad blood brewed.

Barrett looked for a way to destroy his competition, and soon he found it. A disagreement between groups of black and white boys over a game of marbles provided a way for Barrett to stir up violence.

The disagreement spread to the boys' fathers, and fights ensued. The police came, but the fights were over by then. Barrett wanted the grocery store owners to be arrested for inciting a riot, but since there was no evidence of a riot, that didn't happen.

Barrett had to try something else. He went to a local judge and claimed that Calvin McDowell had assaulted him with a pistol and mallet. Any assaulting was likely done by Barrett, but McDowell was bigger and had gotten the best of the grocer in the scuffle. Before any-

thing could be settled about the marbles incident, African Americans held a meeting to discuss the issue. Barrett went to the judge again and persuaded him to issue arrest warrants for two of the inflammatory speakers who had supposedly tried to rouse the black population against whites.

The People's Grocery was outside of the Memphis city limits, so Barrett contacted the county sheriff, who agreed to send deputies to arrest the accused inflammatory speakers. At the same time, Barrett spread a rumor that a white mob was going to destroy the store on Saturday night.

Moss and his partners talked to a lawyer, who told them that they could legally protect their property since they were outside the city limits. McDowell, Stewart, and several friends armed themselves and waited at the store late on Saturday night.

Meanwhile, the sheriff deputized several citizens, making them temporary deputies. These deputies along with Barrett and several other men broke into the store through the back door to arrest the inflammatory speakers. They didn't wear badges or uniforms and didn't announce themselves as deputies. The men in the store thought they were being attacked by a mob and opened fire.

A panoramic view of downtown Memphis in 1910

Three men were wounded and the rest fled. The three wounded men turned out to be the deputies. It took only hours for all of Memphis to hear the distorted story that Barrett and the others told. The newspapers magnified the incident into a bloody ambush of several lawmen. Rumors spread that African Americans were getting ready to stage a huge uprising against whites.

Gangs of whites surged into the Curve area, looted the People's Grocery, and broke into black people's homes. Thirty black men who were identified as conspirators in the ambush were arrested. Moss was arrested along with McDowell and Stewart. The trio knew that they hadn't done anything wrong and expected to be released as soon as everything was straightened out. They felt more confident after the papers announced that the three wounded deputies were recovering.

43

For two nights, the jail was guarded by the Tennessee Rifles, an African American militia unit. Then the judge ordered that all blacks in Memphis and surrounding areas be disarmed, including the Tennessee Rifles. Members of this black state militia unit protested to local and state authorities, noting their prior service to the state, but the disarming order stood. The Tennessee Rifles disbanded their unit in disgust and never met again.

The jailed prisoners were left unguarded except for the jailers. Two nights later, a white mob descended on the jail and dragged the three store owners out of their cells. They were taken out of town and shot to death. The newspapers reported that Moss had begged for his life for the sake of his family, but seeing that he was going to be shot, said: "Tell my people to go west—there is no justice for them here."

The African American community in Memphis was outraged by the killings. The white newspapers painted the store owners as thugs, even though the three had been hardworking Memphis citizens. The jailer claimed that he had been overpowered by at least thirty men, who swept into his jail and snatched the prisoners. It was later noted that there may have been ten men, and there was minimal resistance from the jailer. He also said that he couldn't identify any members of the mob, but that was probably a lie, as well.

Lynching wasn't new to the South or to the rest of the country. Lynchings had been reported since colonial days. In pre-Revolutionary America, lynchings were often beatings rather than killings, and British sympathizers were the usual targets. The punishment was always outside of the law, and this particular brand of lynching practically disappeared after the Revolution.

Lynching was identified mostly with the frontier in America, whether that was western Pennsylvania or Kentucky. Residents of frontier towns saw lynching as a way to administer justice in areas where law enforcement was new or weak.

Whites were much more likely to be targets in frontier towns. Blacks were usually slaves and as such had monetary value to their owners. A slave owner wouldn't willingly allow his property to be destroyed.

The exception would be if the owner was afraid of slave rebellion. Black lynchings took place more often as the nineteenth century progressed for this very reason. Slaveholders were fearful of slave uprisings because often there were so many more blacks than whites on the plantations. They were willing to occasionally sacrifice a slave or two to lynching to keep the others in line.

Lynching of blacks in the South gradually increased up through the Civil War and Reconstruction, and it became almost epidemic by the 1890s. However, reasons for lynching had changed by 1890. As African Americans were increasingly restricted by Jim Crow (segregation) laws and saw their political power wane, the possibility of black insurrection no longer seemed imminent to southern whites. But lynching continued and increased in spite of this seeming lessening of a threat. The one reason trumpeted throughout the South was that black men were attacking and raping white women. Southerners were united in their condemnation of the awful crimes allegedly being committed against white women, and felt they couldn't do less than hunt down and kill the criminals. As Ida would discover, this was far from the whole story behind the increase in lynchings.

Ida was in Natchez on newspaper business when the lynching of the three men occurred. She didn't return until after the funeral had been held for Thomas Moss and the others. Ida was heartbroken to hear of the deaths of Moss and his partners. Moss had been a good friend of Ida's, and she was the godmother of the Moss's young daughter, Maurine. Betty Moss was pregnant with her second child at the time of the lynching. Ida said of the Mosses: "He and his wife Betty were the best friends I had in town. And he believed, with me, that we should defend the cause of right and fight wrong wherever we saw it."

Within days, Moss's last words of advice for his race were being talked about in every African American home. Soon people were heeding his advice to go west. They loaded up their belongings and moved out of Memphis. The *Free Speech* added its voice to the go-west cry. In the lead article, Ida wrote: "There is therefore only one thing left that we can do; save our money and leave a town which will neither protect our lives and property, nor give us a fair trial in the courts, but takes us out and murders us in cold blood when accused by white persons."

Some blacks moved across the Mississippi River to Arkansas, and others moved to the Oklahoma Territory and Kansas. Many moved out of the South altogether. Migration out of Memphis had been happening before the lynchings, but it became a flood afterward. Ida took a three-week trip to check out Oklahoma in early April 1892. She wrote letters home that were published in the *Free Speech*. She expressed what she saw there and discussed the opportunities for blacks in Oklahoma.

Within six weeks of the lynchings, the white Memphis population was feeling an economic squeeze. However bigoted the white's view of African Americans was, blacks still formed a large portion of the labor force in Memphis. They also spent their money on goods and services that were largely provided by white businesses.

Ida reported in the *Free Speech* that representatives of the local streetcar company had come to her to ask that she reassure blacks that it was safe to ride their newly electrified streetcars. They assumed that fear of the electricity had kept blacks from riding streetcars. Ida knew differently. She pointed out that the sudden loss of business happened right after the lynchings. Company officials insisted that the streetcar company had nothing to do with the killings so that shouldn't have affected their business.

In reply, Ida wrote of Thomas Moss: "A finer, cleaner man than he never walked the streets of Memphis. He was well liked, a favorite with everybody; yet he was murdered with no more consideration than if he had been a dog, because he as a man defended his property from attack. The colored people feel that every white man in Memphis who consented to his death is as guilty as those who fired the guns which took his life, and they want to get away from this town."

The weeks after her friend's lynching set Ida's life on a different course. Her writings up until then had focused mostly on segregation's expansion and on the declining political power of blacks. That would all change as a result of the personal stake she felt in Thomas Moss's death.

Ida began a research project after Moss was lynched that would continue for years. First she read old newspaper accounts of lynchings throughout the South, looking at both white- and black-owned papers for the cause given for the lynchings. She probably expected to find that Moss's lynching was out of the ordinary, coming as it did without any accusation of rape. She was stunned to find that rape was not even charged in at least two-thirds of the lynchings reported.

Ida wrote about the effect that this discovery had on her view of lynching's causes:

Ida (left) and the family of Thomas Moss:
daughter Maurine, wife Betty, and Thomas Moss Jr.

> Like many another person who had read of lynching in the South, I had accepted the idea meant to be conveyed—that although lynching was irregular and contrary to law and order, unreasoning anger over the terrible crime of rape led to the lynching; that perhaps the brute deserved to die anyhow and the mob was justified in taking his life. But Thomas Moss, Calvin McDowell, and Lee Stewart had been lynched . . . with just as much brutality as other victims of the mob; and they had committed no crime against white women. This is what opened my eyes to what lynching really was. An excuse to get rid of Negroes who were acquiring wealth and property and thus keep the race terrorized and 'keep the nigger down.'

Ida filled the *Free Speech* with anti-lynching articles in the weeks after Moss's death. As her certainty grew that lynching was designed to keep her race from being successful rather than as a way to punish rape, her articles became more heated.

At last she wrote the editorial that would spell the end of her career in Memphis and the beginning of a new life in the North. As she prepared to go on a planned trip to Philadelphia for the American Methodist Episcopal Church general conference, Ida wrote her editorials in advance. She was in Philadelphia at the conference when the following appeared in the May 21, 1892, edition of the *Free Speech*.

> Eight Negroes lynched since last issue of the *Free Speech*. Three were charged with killing white men and five with raping white women. Nobody in this section believes the old thread-bare lie that Negro men assault white women. If Southern white men are not careful they will over-reach themselves and a conclusion will be reached which will be very damaging to the moral reputation of their women.

The uproar was immediate, and turmoil once again engulfed Memphis. The conclusion that Ida spoke of was that black men and white women were falling in love with each other. This idea was appalling to any white southern man and could drive him to violence.

It's likely that Ida had a good idea what an uproar her editorial would stir up, although she may not have foreseen the level of hatred it produced. At first, Memphis residents thought that J. L. Fleming, Ida's remaining partner after Reverend Nightingale had retired, had written the offensive words. One of the city's white newspapers, the *Memphis Commercial*, called the editor a scoundrel and implied that violence might be needed to straighten things out. Another local paper bluntly called for the author to be tied to a stake and branded on the forehead.

There were more editorials, and whites held an angry meeting to denounce the *Free Speech*. They appointed a committee to go to the newspaper offices. Luckily, Fleming was warned and left town ahead of the mob. Reports differ as to what the committee actually did, but Ida wrote later that the printing type and furnishings were destroyed and a warning was posted. The *New York Sun* reported that a death threat was posted against anyone who tried to publish the paper again.

Ida was oblivious to the happenings in Memphis until after the church conference ended. When she traveled to New York City for the second leg of her trip, T. Thomas Fortune met her at the train station. According to Ida, Fortune said upon greeting her: "Well, we've been a long time getting you to New York, but now you are here I am afraid you will have to stay."

> "If Southern white men are not careful they will over-reach themselves and a conclusion will be reached which will be very damaging to the moral reputation of their women."
>
> Ida B. Wells

When Ida expressed doubt, Fortune said: "Well, from the rumpus you have kicked up I feel assured of it. Oh, I know it was you because it sounded just like you." With that he handed her a copy of the *New York Sun* with its report of the events in Memphis.

Ida's first reaction was to telegraph her lawyer in Memphis, B. F. Booth, to see if Fleming was safe. After receiving assurances that Fleming has escaped, Ida contemplated what she should do next. She thought that she could probably safely return to Memphis because she was a woman and a longtime city resident. However, a series of telegrams from Booth and other friends convinced her otherwise.

Friends reported that unidentified white men had been looking for Ida, and that Ida's house was being watched as were the incoming trains. It was rumored that white men had vowed to kill Ida on sight. Ida's friends said that there were black men who would protect her should she return to Memphis, but they advised her to stay away and avoid more bloodshed.

Ida decided to stay in New York and begin a new life there. It would be a life devoted to ridding the country of lynching as a means of keeping her people in their place.

# FIVE

## *England to Chicago*

In June 1892, Ida found herself in New York City without a home or job but with a story to tell. Fortune and his co-editor, Jerome Peterson, immediately offered Ida a one-fourth interest in their paper, the *New York Age*, in return for her subscription lists for the *Free Speech*. She would also write articles for their paper and be paid a salary.

Ida's first article for the *New York Age* was splashed across the front page of the paper on June 25, 1892. The article repeated the editorial that had caused the closing of the *Free Speech*, and Ida also quoted from white-owned newspapers, which would prove to be one of her most effective techniques for years to come.

Ida's strong words did not go unheard in Memphis or in other cities across the country. Fortune printed 10,000 copies of that issue of the *New York Age*, and at least 1,000 were sold in Memphis. The *Memphis Appeal-Avalanche*, a white newspaper, reported in its June 30, 1892, issue that Ida had gone to New York to work for a paper called the *New York Age*, in which "she has continued to publish matter not a whit less scandalous than that which aroused the ire of the whites just prior to her departure."

Ida may have been run out of Memphis, but she didn't go quietly. Indeed, Memphis city fathers may have wished that they hadn't allowed her to gain a national audience by letting her be scared away. She continued to write for the *New York Age*, giving spirited accounts of the lynchings that happened almost daily, as recorded by the *Chicago Daily Tribune*. The year 1892 turned out to be the most deadly yet for lynchings, with 292 recorded deaths by year's end.

Ida worried that the white press was not covering the anti-lynching story enough to get the word out to the whites who might have the power to enact changes. But she did find help in her efforts from two black women from New York: "About two months after my appearance in the columns in the *New York Age*, two colored women remarked on my revelations during a visit with each other and said they thought that the women of New York and Brooklyn should do something to show appreciation of my work and to protest the treatment which I had received."

Victoria Earle Matthews and Maritcha Lyons organized a series of meetings for their friends and acquaintances. Attendance at the meetings grew quickly, and at last a testimonial to Ida was planned for October 5, 1892, at Lyric Hall in New York City. The well-planned event attracted many of the leading black women from New York and Brooklyn, as well as large delegations from Boston and Philadelphia.

Ida was both thrilled and terrified. She understood the importance of reaching this particular audience as a way to expand her influence. However, this would be her first real speech about lynching, and she wasn't sure she could do it successfully. Ida had taken public speaking instructions back in Memphis (which were then called elocution lessons), and she often had given recitations at the lyceum and talks asking for newspaper subscriptions. "But," Ida wrote, "this was the first time I had ever been called on to deliver an honest-to-goodness address."

Ida wrote out her speech even though she said that "every detail of that horrible lynching affair was imprinted on my memory." She felt that the right approach to her audience was to give a sincere but largely unemotional recounting of the story. Ida wanted them to focus on the facts and not her part in the event. But as Ida began to read her address, she couldn't help feeling overwhelmed with sadness for the lynching itself and loneliness due to leaving behind her friends in Memphis. She felt the tears coming.

"A panic seized me," Ida recounted later. "I was afraid that I was going to make a scene and spoil all that those dear good women had done for me. I kept saying to myself that whatever happened I must not break down, and so I kept on reading." Tears trickled down Ida's face, but she continued to read her speech, stopping only to mop at the tears with a handkerchief. By the time she was finished, she was sure she had disappointed her benefactors by her show of weakness.

It was soon apparent that the women in attendance felt differently. Ida wrote that "the women didn't feel that I had spoiled things by my breakdown. They seemed to think that it had made an impression on the audience favorable to the cause and me."

That did seem to be the result, as speaking invitations flooded in to Ida over the following months. She also used the money raised by the testimonial to publish a pamphlet version of the June *New York Age* article. Titled *Southern Horrors, Lynch Law in All Its Phases*, the pamphlet carried an introduction by Frederick Douglass. The famous Douglass lent authority to Ida's words as he praised her efforts on behalf of their race. "Let me give you thanks for your faithful paper on the lynch abomination now generally practiced against colored people in the South," he wrote. "There has been no word equal to it in convincing power."

Ida wrote in the pamphlet preface: "It is with no pleasure I have dipped my hands in the corruption here exposed. Somebody must show that the Afro-American race is more sinned against than sinning, and it seems to have fallen upon me to do so."

The pamphlet related the lynching at the Curve in Memphis and went on to systematically cite examples of brutality against blacks, as the June *New York Age* article had done. Ida expanded the pamphlet, adding more examples, since her research had continued throughout the summer.

Frederick Douglass

According to Ida, evidence suggested that white women sometimes invited attention from black men. She told of a minister's wife in Ohio who had accused a black man of rape. William Offett was convicted and sent to prison in December 1888 for fifteen years. Several years later, the wife confessed to her husband that she had invited the relationship. The minister had Offett released and divorced his wife.

Another white woman, the wife of a doctor, ran away with their black coachman. Sarah Clark of Memphis, according to Ida, lived with a black man and, when arrested for that offense, said she was not a white woman. Yet another young white woman of Memphis stole money from her father to allow her black lover to escape her father's wrath.

After showing that white women were not always the victims, Ida went on to report—using published newspaper accounts—case after case of lynching in which the victims' guilt was strongly in doubt or totally unproven. She wrote of lynchings that were completely unrelated to any rape charge, including "the case of the boy Will Lewis who was hanged at Tullahoma, Tennessee, last year (1891) for being drunk and sassy to white folks."

Ida reminded readers that crimes against black women perpetrated by white men went almost completely unpunished. She offered several examples, including one that happened in Baltimore, Maryland. A young African American girl was walking with a young man of her own race when three white men assaulted the couple and raped the girl. The case was tried, and the men were acquitted.

And finally she wrote of the way law officers and even politicians aided in the lynchings of innocent African Americans. Sheriffs and jailers often allowed mobs to beat down the doors of jails and sometimes participated in the lynchings. According to Ida in her article, "Governor Tillman, of South Carolina, in the month of June, standing under the tree in Barnwell, South Carolina, on which eight Afro-Americans were hung last year, declared that he would lead a mob to lynch a Negro who raped a white woman."

Ida spoke to multiple groups in the months after *Southern Horrors* was published. She was well-received in Philadelphia, Boston, and Washington, to name a few of the cities she visited to proclaim her anti-lynching message. A particularly gruesome lynching that happened in Paris, Texas, in early February 1893 gave new strength and attention to Ida's crusade.

A black man, Henry Smith, had been accused of assaulting and murdering a four-year-old white girl in Paris. Huge crowds of white onlookers gathered to watch as he was placed on a scaffold and tortured with red-hot irons and eventually burned alive. Special excursion trains had brought people from the surrounding areas to view the spectacle. Members of the crowd fought over bones and teeth found in the hot ashes. They wanted the remains as souvenirs of the event.

Smith died protesting his innocence, and without a trial there was no way to prove anything. With the money given to her for a speaking fee, Ida hired a Pinkerton detective to gather the facts on the case,

An estimated 10,000 people gathered to witness the lynching of Henry Smith in Paris, Texas, in 1893. The *New York Times* covered the hanging and its headline read, "Another Negro Burned. Henry Smith Dies at the Stake. Drawn Through the Streets on a Car—Tortured For Nearly an Hour and Then Burned—Awful Vengeance of a Paris (Texas) Mob."

although all he did was send her newspaper clippings. Later in her career, she would use the same investigative technique with better results.

The horrible actions of the mob when they lynched Henry Smith brought public attention from around the world. Ida's dramatic words were apt. "The fire lighted by this human torch flamed round the world," she wrote.

Two women in England did more than just shake their heads in disgust over Smith's shocking death. Catherine Impey was the editor of a publication called *Anti-Caste*, which championed the cause of non-whites, particularly in India. Isabelle Mayo was a Scottish author who also worked against the caste system in India. Impey had recently traveled in the U.S. and, knowing that, Mayo invited her to Scotland to confer on the causes of such an outrage. Wells said that Mayo asked Impey if "she had learned, when in America the year before, why the United States of America was burning human beings alive in the nineteenth century as the red Indians were said to have done three hundred years before."

Impey had no ready answer, so Mayo proposed that they get someone to come from the United States to talk to them about it. Soon a plan was made to bring Ida to England to help Mayo and Impey launch a new movement that would campaign against all the evils of caste throughout the world. Lynching in America would be their first target because they deemed it the most urgent cause.

On April 5, 1893, Ida sailed to England for a speaking tour. She was intensely aware that this trip could catapult her anti-lynching campaign onto the international stage. "It seemed like an open door in a stone wall," Ida wrote of the invitation.

Frederick Douglass had obtained tremendous support from the English for his abolitionist causes before the Civil War. Ida hoped it could be the same for her. She needed the white newspapers in the U.S. to pay attention to her crusade because the papers could mold public opinion.

Ida's ship docked in Liverpool on April 19, and from there she journeyed to Impey's home in Somerset. After a short rest, the pair went to Mayo's home in Aberdeen in northern Scotland. From there the three women set out on a speaking tour. Ida gave public lectures in Aberdeen, Huntly, and Edinburgh. When a public address wasn't scheduled, she spoke to small groups in private homes.

Impey left to arrange meetings in England, and soon after an uproar arose. Impey had written a letter to a co-worker of Isabelle Mayo, Dr. George Ferdinands, indicating that her feelings for him were romantic in nature. Dr. Ferdinands, who boarded with Mayo, was the son of a British father and Ceylonese mother. He had helped with the plans for Ida's tour. Apparently, Dr. Ferdinands was shocked by Impey's declaration and showed the letter to Mayo, which turned out to be an unwise decision.

Mayo took great offense at what she thought was wildly inappropriate behavior from Impey. Impey had advised Dr. Ferdinands that she was ready to tell her family that she was in love with a man of a darker race and that she was prepared to marry him. The romantic nature of the letter came under question because Impey had stated how happy she would be to prove to the world that her theories about the equality of mankind were more than just talk.

Ida found herself in the middle of a huge fight, as Mayo declared that Impey must be ousted from the new society the two had formed to promote the brotherhood of man. Mayo insisted that Ida must withdraw from working with Impey because Mayo was quite sure that the lovesick lady would eventually disgrace their efforts.

Ida was torn between the two women. Ida didn't approve of Impey's behavior, but she saw no reason that anyone besides Dr. Ferdinands and the three women should ever know of the incident. After much agonizing and prayer, Ida told Mayo that she couldn't abandon Impey because of all the woman had done to help Ida's cause. Mayo was unmoved by Ida's pleas for understanding and cut all ties with both Impey and Wells.

Ida proceeded on her speaking tour, with Impey as the guide. Ida regretted the loss of Mayo's influence in gaining engagements, but there were still many successful appearances. British newspapers gave largely favorable reviews to Ida's speeches. This in turn attracted attention from American newspapers.

The *Memphis Appeal-Avalanche* reported to its readers that "Ida Wells is continuing her career of triumphant mendacity." The writer felt that the English were hearing only one side of the lynching story and that was the one of "the negro adventuress who has so deftly gulled a number of credulous persons in England." The paper denied it supported lynch law but went on to state that lynching often resulted "only when the African Americans have, by their crimes, stirred up the people beyond all restraint."

Other white newspapers in America labeled Ida a racist because she crusaded only against the lynching of blacks and not the lynching of whites. The *Washington Post* declared that Ida was mistaken when she said that Americans didn't care that mob law was the only law when it came to black lynchings. The paper said that opposition was strong, although it did not say where this opposition was found.

Ida didn't like being criticized at any time during her life, but this kind of criticism was helpful to her cause because it stirred public opinion. It appeared that her English tour was accomplishing for Ida what she hadn't been able to do in America. People were listening and thinking about what she said even if they insisted on disagreeing.

Ida sailed home at the end of May after the invitations to speak ceased. She felt that her trip had been quite successful, but Impey was convinced that the trouble with Mayo had practically ruined the tour. Whatever the true outcome, Ida was convinced of the necessity to influence world opinion. A new opportunity to do so was happening in Chicago that summer.

The Chicago World's Fair, or Columbian Exposition, had been scheduled to take place in 1892, but the buildings weren't finished in time. The fair opened officially on May 1, 1893, and ran until October of the same year. More than 27 million people attended the celebration of Columbus's landing in America in 1492. The fair included exhibits from all over the world, including six large buildings with white Italian classical facades.

What was glaringly missing from the fair was any representation of blacks other than ones depicting African tribes as backward people. African American leaders had lobbied to be included either in separate exhibits or in common with white Americans. Frederick Douglass tried to use his influence, but the commission in charge wasn't interested in presenting any exhibits that didn't celebrate white economic and moral superiority.

Before Ida's trip abroad, she had joined with Douglass and Frederick J. Loudin to propose that a pamphlet be created and circulated to fair attendees. Douglass and Loudin didn't have much success getting donations to fund the project while Ida was gone, and Ida had limited success when she returned. Finally, they decided to scale back their plans and publish the pamphlet only in English rather than in English, French, German, and Spanish as originally planned. They would include prefaces in French and German.

The pamphlet was entitled *The Reason Why the Colored American Is Not in the World's Columbian Exposition*. Ida was the driving force

An interior view of an exhibit hall (right) at the 1893 Chicago World's Fair, and an exterior view of the exposition grounds (below)

behind the pamphlet, but several people contributed. Frederick Douglass wrote the introduction and two chapters, and Ferdinand L. Barnett, a lawyer whom Ida would marry in 1895, wrote a chapter that told how African American leaders had tried to be included in the exposition. Prominent black editor I. Garland Penn also wrote one chapter, and Ida penned the one on lynching.

The pamphlets were to be handed out at the Haitian Building Exhibit, which the Haitian government had asked Douglass to supervise. Douglass had served as minister to Haiti from 1889 to 1891 and was deeply respected by the Haitians. Ida passed out most of the pamphlets, which were finished in mid-August.

The pamphlet project went smoothly enough once the fund-raising difficulties were overcome, but another fair project caused a serious disagreement between Douglass and Wells. In a compromise move, the Exposition Committee had asked Douglass to plan a "Colored Jubilee Day" that would celebrate African Americans. Other nationalities also had their days, but Ida thought a jubilee day was a terrible idea. She believed it would be in poor taste and certainly not dignified.

Frederick Douglass, however, thought it was a splendid plan. He proceeded to put together a program of music, speeches, and poetry that was widely reported on across the United States. Ida didn't even attend the fair that day. But after reading the newspaper coverage the next day, she was so impressed with Douglass's event that she "went straight out to the fair and begged his pardon for presuming in my youth and inexperience to criticize him for an effort which had done more to bring our cause to the attention of the American people than anything else which had happened at the fair."

## MISS IDA B. WELLS

Informs Our Readers as to the Condition of the World's Fair Pamphlet Movement.

What the Pamphlet Will Be—The Amount of Cash in Hand and Subscribed—Ohio Afro-Americans Should Do Their Duty at Once and Forward Something to Aid the Movement.

Special to THE GAZETTE.

EDITOR GAZETTE:—So many write to ask me to send them an explanation of what the world's fair pamphlet is intended for, that I beg space to say in a few words what we are trying to do.

There is no appropriation for stamps, secretary, etc., hence it comes very hard to answer every personal letter I get on the subject.

It was thought that as the intelligence, skill and every civilized people on the globe was to be represented at the fair, and that many would come expecting to see something of the Afro-American; that as he had been so studiously kept out of representation in any official capacity and given menial places, it was the race's duty to tell why this is so. Especially does this seem necessary when the foreigner, knowing nothing about the kind of prejudice prevailing in this country, will be told all manner of things to the Afro-American's discredit as a race by the white American. The pamphlet is intended as a calm, dignified statement of the Afro-American's side of the story, from the beginning to the present day; a recital of the obstacles which have hampered him; a sketch of what he has done in twenty-five years with all his persecution, and a statement of the fruitless efforts he made for representation at the world's fair.

Ida had been drawn to Chicago by the opportunities the Columbian Exposition presented for her to gain worldwide attention for her anti-lynching crusade. When it was over, she decided to live in Chicago. The city had a growing African American population partly because an Illinois civil rights law guaranteed equal access to all public accommodations. There was a vibrant social and cultural life for blacks in the city, which attracted many literate migrants, especially from Tennessee and Kentucky.

Ida accepted an offer from the *Chicago Conservator*, a black newspaper edited by R. P. Bird and owned by Ferdinand L. Barnett. She then settled down to make Chicago her home, although the next year and a half would find her on the road much of the time.

Ida informs readers about the World's Fair Pamphlet Movement in this July 22, 1893, article in the *Cleveland Gazette*.

# SIX

## *Travels for the Cause*

In September 1893, Ida received an invitation to make another speaking tour in England. Isabelle Mayo had sent the invitation to Ida on behalf of the council of the organization that she and Catherine Impey had founded, the Society for the Recognition of the Brotherhood of Man (SRBM). S. J. Edwards edited the SRBM publication, *Fraternity*. Edwards would make all the tour arrangements and generally be in charge of the months-long event.

Ida consented, but even before she left there was trouble with Mayo regarding Impey. Mayo still wanted Ida to publicly denounce Impey, which Ida would not do. She considered canceling the trip, but Edwards assured her that the SRBM Council only wanted her to be quiet about the dispute. With this reassurance and the promise of ample financial support, Ida left for England in late February 1894.

Ida had barely landed in Liverpool on March 9 when Mayo announced that she was withdrawing her financial support for Ida's tour. It seems she hadn't known that the SRBM Council through Edwards had told Ida that it wasn't necessary for her to reject Impey publicly.

As if that wasn't a hard enough blow for Ida, she also discovered that Edwards was seriously ill and wouldn't be able to take care of the arrangements for Ida's tour.

While trying to figure out what to do, Ida went ahead and gave her first address two days later. She delivered it with style and flare at the Pembroke Chapel in Liverpool. The pastor at Pembroke, Charles Aked, liked Ida and, hearing of her difficulties, asked her to stay with him and his wife until the tour arrangements could be straightened out. The Akeds became close friends of Ida's, and their home remained her base of operations for the whole time she was in England. Aked suggested that Ida write to Frederick Douglass for a recommendation. He reasoned that a letter from the famous abolitionist might open some doors for Ida in England.

Aked was correct, but the request for a letter of recommendation brought about yet another disagreement with Douglass. He replied to Ida's request with a somewhat uninspired recommendation letter that he sent to Aked and a rather miffed one to Ida. "Will you oblige me by telling me frankly who invited you to spend three months in England and what assurances they gave you of support while on this mission?" Douglass wrote to Ida. He added: "[I]f you have not been invited and have gone to England on your own motion and for your own purposes, you should have frankly told me so."

Douglass may have received letters about Ida from Mayo or perhaps had wearied of the young woman's trouble. Moreover, Wells had borrowed money from Douglass and had not paid the loan. Whatever the reason for Douglass's response, Ida was devastated by his words. She wrote to him: "I have never felt so like giving up as since I received your very cool and cautious letter this morning, with its tone of distrust and its inference that I have not dealt truthfully with you."

In spite of the early difficulties, Ida's speaking tour was a raging success, and she also managed to repair the rift with Douglass. She gave more than a hundred lectures in less than five months and was interviewed many times. More than fifty accounts of her activities and speeches appeared in British newspapers. Almost all of the press attention was positive for her and her cause.

During her tour, Ida sent long articles back to the white-owned newspaper Chicago *Inter-Ocean* about the talks she gave in various English cities and the response her talks received. The *Inter-Ocean* was paying her a small amount to be a correspondent for them while in Europe. These articles—plus the ones she sent back to her own paper, the *Conservator*,

A 1901 photo of the ocean steamship landing in Liverpool, England

and Fortune's paper, the *New York Age*—caused the same stir in the American press as her previous trip's accounts had.

The Memphis papers were particularly biting in their responses to Ida's stories of her English travels. That might be expected since Ida continued to use the Memphis lynchings of March 1892 as the centerpiece of her talks. She also used newer information, but Thomas Moss's lynching was her personal stake in the issue.

The May 26, 1894, issue of the *Memphis Commercial Appeal* viciously criticized Wells. Among other equally distasteful descriptions, the paper called Ida a "disreputable colored woman, intriguing adventuress, malicious wanton and infamous slanderer."

The Liverpool paper said it couldn't reprint the *Commercial* article or another by the *Memphis Appeal-Avalanche* because both articles "are very coarse in tone, and some of the language is such as could not possibly be reproduced in an English journal."

Ida used the nastiness of the Memphis papers' articles to her benefit when she wrote about them in one of her articles for the *Inter-Ocean*.

She wrote that if she was being called an "adventuress" for stating the facts of lynching, what should those who ignore the facts be called? She continued: "However revolting these lynchings, I did not commit a single one of them, nor could the wildest effort of my imagination manufacture one to equal their reality."

English newspapers characterized Ida as a cultured woman who dressed well and had great charm. These appealing traits helped her as she spread her anti-lynching crusade throughout Britain.

Ida waged one more battle while in England when she challenged Frances Willard, the American president of the Women's Christian Temperance (anti-alcohol) Union (WCTU). The WCTU was active in England, and Willard was touring there at the same time as Ida.

Frances Willard

Willard had made some unfortunate remarks about blacks in an interview in the *New York Voice* in 1890. She had said that lynching was a crime, but of blacks she said: "The colored race multiplies like the locusts of Egypt. The grog-shop is its center of power."

Willard had been on tour in the South at the time of the interview and was playing to her audience in order to capture their support for her temperance cause. When questioned about Willard, Ida gave her opinion that Willard was far from being an active anti-lynching supporter.

The article on Willard surfaced again when Ida gave it to the *Fraternity* for publication shortly after she arrived back in England. Ida said that she knew she would face questions about Willard on her tour and wanted to get the facts out. It's possible that she hoped to stir up more interest in her own cause. Willard was much revered in England, and a controversy over her words would attract attention.

When speaking, Ida quoted from Willard's article and added her own comments about the temperance leader's apparent views on blacks. Lady Isabel Somerset, Willard's prominent English sponsor and friend, got wind of the *Fraternity* article before it was published and was furious. Somerset wrote an angry letter to Frederick Douglass and conducted her own interview with Willard, which would be published before the *Fraternity* piece.

There's evidence that Willard had changed her mind about lynching and some of its causes after that 1890 interview, but she never totally denounced the idea that black men were somehow to blame for their own fates. As she often did, Ida had used a white's own words to illustrate the need for reform.

Ida's second tour of England ended on a triumphant note, as she helped organize the London Anti-Lynching Committee. A large group of prominent English men and women gathered for a social evening at the home of P. W. Clayden, where Ida was staying. Clayden was the editor of the *London Daily News*. At the end of the evening, they gathered to organize their new committee. The Duke of Argyle, son-in-law of Queen Victoria, was named president, and members included many editors, college professors, members of Parliament, and other notables. The committee would raise money to work against lynching and the disregard for the law it represented.

Ida sailed for home soon after and arrived to a rousing welcome in New York City on July 24, 1894. Both white and black press representatives were on hand, and their papers published complimentary accounts of Ida and her crusade. An equally exciting celebration was held in Brooklyn. Ida talked about her experiences overseas and how the English had supported her campaign. She appealed to Americans to do likewise, and wrote, "I thought that it was up to us to show that we could do as much for ourselves as they had done for us, that if they [her audience] would be responsible for raising the necessary funds for the expenses of traveling, and personal needs, I would gladly donate another year to the cause."

Ida optimistically hoped that an organization could be successfully started in the U.S. to fund a nationwide anti-lynching crusade. But the necessary contributions never came, and Ida was forced to support her own efforts the best way she could. Ida soon began to receive invitations to speak from all over the country. She remained hopeful that the anti-lynching support would build into a network, which would fund her travels, but meanwhile she started on her promised year-long tour. She charged fees for her lectures and used the money to pay her traveling expenses.

Ida visited dozens of northern, eastern, and western cities, including St. Louis, Des Moines, Kansas City, Omaha, Denver, and Los Angeles. Her message remained the same, with the addition of details about any new lynchings reported. She spoke mostly to black clubs and churches, large and small, but occasionally a white church invited her to talk.

Ida's tour during 1894 and 1895 was probably the high point of her anti-lynching crusade. The press, both white and black, covered her travels extensively and generally gave her positive reviews. After hearing Ida speak, the groups that comprised her audiences often passed resolutions supporting her and her anti-lynching activities. Sometimes they formed local anti-lynching leagues and carried on her work after she left.

During her travels, Ida somehow found time to work on another pamphlet, which was published in early 1895. *The Red Record* listed lynching victims and the alleged crimes for the years 1893 and 1894. Most of the pamphlet told story after story of brutal lynchings, but it included one chapter about Ida's quarrel with Frances Willard.

In the conclusion of *The Red Record*, Ida repeated the remedy to stop lynching that she used throughout her crusade. "The very frequent inquiry made after my lectures by interested friends is 'What can I do to help the cause?' The answer always is: 'Tell the world the facts.'

Susan B. Anthony

When the Christian world knows the alarming growth and extent of outlawry in our land, some means will be found to stop it."

Ida remained convinced that the majority of whites and some blacks simply did not know the truth about lynching. Her yearlong tour was devoted to spreading this truth.

Ida often shared the stage with other famous reformers, including Douglass and women's suffrage leader Susan B. Anthony. Ida appeared with Douglass at a huge meeting in November 1894 in Providence, Rhode Island. That turned out to be the last time she saw Douglass; he died unexpectedly on February 20, 1895. Ida was speaking in San Francisco and could not go east for his funeral.

Ida helped organize a memorial service in San Francisco that was covered widely in the newspapers there. She wrote later of the words she had spoken at the memorial: "I was the chief speaker and voiced the sentiments which I have never yet changed, that in the death of Frederick Douglass we lost the greatest man that the Negro race has ever produced on the American continent."

In April 1895, Ida was a house guest of Susan B. Anthony's in Rochester, New York, while Ida spoke there. Ida greatly admired the determined suffragist, although the two didn't always agree. Anthony tried unsuccessfully to make Ida see that it was sometimes necessary to make concessions to prejudice to serve the greater cause. Anthony also expressed that much injustice in America would cease once women got the vote. Ida was not optimistic about that.

One of Ida's most vivid memories was that Anthony fired her stenographer when the woman refused to take dictation from Ida because she was black. To Ida, this action showed better than any words could that Anthony opposed segregation and its vile effects.

By summer 1895, Ida was exhausted and ready to return to Chicago. She had crisscrossed the country on speaking tours dozens of

times, had made friends and enemies, and had done it with only the money she earned from her lecture fees. She said of the end of her tour: "I felt that I had done all

Ferdinand Barnett

that one human being could do in trying to keep the matter before the public in my country and in trying to find that righteous public sentiment, which would help to put an end to these terrible lynchings."

But Ida wasn't returning to Chicago only to resume her old life as a newspaper editor. "So, when I at last came back to Chicago, in June 1895, it was to accept the offer of a home of my own which had been made to me before my last trip to England."

Ida was referring obliquely to Ferdinand's proposal of marriage. Ferdinand and Ida had worked together on the Columbian Exposition pamphlet in 1893, and their friendship led to a long-distance courtship. Ferdinand must have proposed to Ida in 1894 before she left on her second trip to England, but she didn't officially accept until late in her nationwide tour of the United States.

Ida's relationships with prospective suitors had often been stormy, especially in her younger days. Ferdinand Barnett seemed the perfect match for her. He respected her talents and ambitions and wasn't intimidated by her feisty personality. They agreed on almost every issue about lynching and black civil rights. Ida could respect Ferdinand yet maintain much of her independence.

The couple was married on June 27, 1895, at Chicago's Bethel A.M.E. Church. The wedding was a major social event with more than five hundred invitations issued to guests, who traveled from all over the U.S. to attend. The Illinois Women's Republican State Central Committee sent word that they would like to attend. Their attendance greatly pleased Ida. She wrote: "These women did attend in a body, accompanied by their husbands, and were dressed in honor of the occasion in evening attire, just the same as if they had attended a wedding among themselves. This we considered a very great honor."

The newlyweds didn't take a honeymoon, and in less than a week Ida took over as editor of her new husband's newspaper, the *Conservator*. Ida purchased the paper from Ferdinand, evidently to preserve her independence. She remained the editor for several years.

Ida curtailed her speaking for a few weeks mostly because she had been so exhausted by her yearlong tour. But soon she was once again giving lectures and working with area women's clubs.

The next spring brought new duties for Ida. As she put it, "I was not too busy to give birth to a male child the following 25 March 1896." The Barnetts' first son was named Charles Aked Barnett after the English clergyman who had been so kind to Ida on her last trip to England.

Ida did not find it necessary to give up her speaking engagements after Charles was born. During the first time that she traveled with him, her husband paid for a nurse to accompany them. After that, Ida required that the groups asking her to speak provide a baby sitter for each event.

The baby sitting arrangement went smoothly with the exception of one occasion. The meeting was in the afternoon, and the nurse asked to be allowed to listen to Ida's speech while caring for Charles. "When the time came for me to speak," Ida recalled, "I rose and went forward. The baby, who was wide awake, looked around, and failing to see me but hearing my voice, raised his voice in angry protest." The chairman jumped up and took the baby out of range of Ida's voice, leaving the nurse to listen to Ida's speech.

In 1896, Ida also helped start a kindergarten in the black section of Chicago. Kindergartens were a new experiment at that time, and the members of the Ida B. Wells Club thought that starting one would be a splendid accomplishment. The club had been founded after the Columbian Exposition by a group of black women who elected Ida as president and named the club after her. The club women undertook various community projects.

Some of the members did not want to give the impression that they were starting a black kindergarten, which would imply segregation. In the end, the club members notified mothers in the neighborhood of Bethel Church of a half-day program of kindergarten educational activities beginning at the church. Nothing was mentioned about the race of the children. The kindergarten received attention in the city newspapers, and Ida was quite pleased with her work on behalf of the education of children.

# SEVEN
## *National Organizations*

The 1890s were a difficult decade for African Americans. Jim Crow laws increasingly restricted their freedoms, disfranchisement proceeded, and lynching continued. Jim Crow laws were named after "Jump Jim Crow," a character in a popular, pre-Civil War minstrel show that stereotyped African Americans. The state and local laws mandated the separation of blacks and whites in many different arenas, including railroads, schools, restaurants, theaters, parks, and hospitals to name just a few.

Ida's voice wasn't the only one to demand attention. In the first half of the decade, dozens of black women's clubs emerged throughout the North, Midwest, and South. Their purposes ranged from community service work to temperance, suffrage, education, and other political issues. Many were organized in honor of Ida after her 1892 speeches. By the middle of the 1890s, the groups began joining in federations, which held national meetings once every year or two.

Soon after her wedding in 1895, Ida was unable to attend a meeting held in Boston. The main reason for the meeting was a nasty editorial against black women issued by John W. Jacks, president of the Missouri Press Association. He wrote it in response to a letter from the British Anti-Lynching Committee, which had asked American journalists for their help in the battle against lynching. He wrote in part: "The African Americans in this country are wholly devoid of morality. The women are prostitutes and all are natural liars and thieves. . . . Out of 200 in this vicinity it is doubtful if there are a dozen virtuous women of that number who are not daily thieving from the white people."

It was hardly the first time that such a venomous attack had been launched against black women, but this time they felt they were able to defend themselves. Accordingly, the Boston Woman's Club, headed by Josephine St. Pierre Ruffin, called for a conference to discuss how to educate the white public about black women.

Ida was absent, but her influence was deeply felt. The group passed a resolution honoring her efforts in her anti-lynching crusade. In spite of their common purposes, delegates still disagreed about tactics. Some of the delegates from Washington, D.C., along with others, were critical of Ida's militant stance and held different opinions than she did about the Women's Christian Temperance Union (WCTU). Ida believed that the WCTU was not forceful enough about condemning lynching.

Margaret Washington

In spite of their disagreements, the women formed the National Federation of Afro-American Women before leaving Boston. The president was Margaret Washington, the wife of famous educator and civil rights leader Booker T. Washington. They planned to meet in Washington, D.C., in the summer of 1896.

The Washington delegates came from an area that boasted eighty-five black women's clubs. Fifteen of the clubs had already formed a national organization that they called the National League of Colored Women. This group also scheduled a meeting for the summer of 1896.

The National League of Colored Women sent a delegation to the federation asking that the two groups negotiate a merger. This time, Ida attended along with four-month-old Charles. Ida was very busy during the convention, as she participated on the resolutions committee and gave a speech on reform. The union of the two organizations was completed successfully with a minimum of conflict. The new organization was called the National Association of Colored Women (NACW).

Many famous women took part in this meeting, including abolitionist Harriet Tubman and Margaret Washington. Mary Church Terrell was elected president of the new organization. Terrell was originally from Memphis and had been acquainted with Ida there. It was Terrell's father, Robert Church, who had lent Ida money for her trip home from California in 1886. Ida had hoped to get to know Terrell then, but Terrell went away to college and the pair's relationship never went beyond acquaintanceship. Later in life, Ida and Terrell were sometimes at odds politically.

Meanwhile, Ida's own family grew as she gave birth to a second son, Herman, in November 1897. "With the birth of my second son," Ida recalled, "all this public work was given up and I retired to the privacy of my home to give my attention to the training of my children." She went on to add: "I felt then, and still feel, that if the mother does not have the training and control of her child's early and most plastic years, she will never gain that control."

Ida's intentions were earnest, but events altered her actions. Lynching and other crimes against African Americans continued and even increased. Ida soon found that she had no choice but to speak out.

Ida's next venture into the national arena came in 1898. In April of that year, a newly appointed black postmaster, Frazier B. Baker, was lynched in Lake City, South Carolina. He was burned to death in his home along with an infant child. African Americans in Chicago were so incensed at the crime that they held a mass meeting. Ida was persuaded to go to Washington to meet with President William McKinley, and a collection was taken to pay her expenses.

Taking five-month-old Herman with her, Ida spent five weeks in the capital lobbying for federal legislation against lynching. Ida, along with several Illinois legislators, did meet with the president. Ida had strong words for McKinley: "To our appeals for justice the stereotyped reply has been that the government could not interfere in a state matter. Postmaster Baker's case was a federal matter, pure and simple. We refuse to believe this country, so powerful to defend its citizens abroad, is unable to protect its citizens at home."

Ida wanted a federal investigation and financial compensation for Baker's family. Ultimately, she wanted federal legislation to outlaw lynching with enough support to see that the law was enforced. President McKinley said that an investigation was underway. Meanwhile, on April 25, 1898, the U.S. declared war on Spain following the sinking of the USS Maine in Havana harbor. The cause of the explosion on the battleship Maine was unclear, but the American press used the incident to call for American intervention in Cuba, publishing slogans such as "Remember the Maine! To hell with Spain!" The brief war ended with the signing of the Treaty of Paris on December 10, 1898—Cuba gained its independence from Spain and Spain ceded the Phillipines, Guam, and Puerto Rico to the U.S. for $20 million. The war may have been the reason that McKinley didn't keep his promise to investigate Baker's case. But Ida suspected that McKinley and the legislators didn't find a compelling reason to proceed.

In September 1898, Ida traveled to another national meeting. The occasion was the revival of the National Afro-American League, which originally had been formed in 1890 by T. Thomas Fortune. Ida had been active in that group while she was a journalist, speaking at the convention in 1891 in Knoxville, Tennessee. In 1893, Fortune had declared the National League dissolved because of lack of funds and indifference by black leaders.

President William McKinley

Fortune was reluctant to revive the league, but he gave in to Bishop Alexander Walters and other prominent black citizens who felt that the deteriorating conditions in the South required a united effort of some sort on the part of black Americans. Fortune had been disillusioned by the previous failure of the black community to support the league and didn't think a revival would produce any better result. He gave in after receiving numerous letters from people wanting to restart it.

Fortune called for a conference of black leaders to be held at the same time that the Frederick Douglass monument was being dedicated in Rochester, New York. The day after the dedication, Ida, Fortune, and other leaders—including Susan B. Anthony and Bishop Walters—met to discuss the proposed revival. The group agreed to form a permanent organization, but Fortune was still not convinced. He was negative about the league's chances of success, saying that black Americans weren't ready for such a movement.

In spite of his outspoken doubt about the organization, Fortune was still elected president of the newly revived league. This decision fired up Ida, who said that Fortune had "spent more time trying to point out the shortcomings of the race than in encouraging us to unite." She also said that Fortune had a "pugnacious attitude."

When the nominating committee's report was put forward for adoption, Ida stopped the process. She later wrote: "I called attention to the fact that Mr. Fortune had said in his morning address that he had no confidence in the race's ability to unite its forces in its own behalf and that he for one was through making sacrifices in its behalf. I wished to know if he planned to accept the presidency of this organization after having made such a declaration."

Fortune promptly resigned. He then nominated Bishop Walters to be president instead. Walters was elected, and Ida became secretary of the organization, which they decided to rename the Afro-American Council.

In December 1898, Bishop Walters called a special meeting to deal with a heightened level of mob violence against African Americans, which had culminated in a race riot in November in Wilmington,

Booker T. Washington

North Carolina. Estimates of deaths of black men range from six to one hundred. Black leaders were upset that President McKinley didn't even mention the riot in an address he made to Congress.

Ida made a heated speech at the Afro-American Council meeting, denouncing the indifference of people in the North to events like the Wilmington riot. She criticized Booker T. Washington for his view that African Americans could win rights by asserting economic power. She criticized President McKinley, who was on a tour through the South at the time of the meeting. She said that "President McKinley was much too interested just now in the national decoration of Confederate graves to pay any attention to the African Americans' rights." Ida was still smarting over McKinley's failure to follow through on the Baker investigation.

This was the first time that Ida spoke publicly of her disagreement with Booker T. Washington's views. In fact, she had praised him at prior meetings. A former slave, Washington had sacrificed much to get an education as a young man and had been appointed president of Tuskegee Institute in Alabama in 1881. Funding for the school was never adequate, and Washington spent many years soliciting money to keep his school afloat. He became acquainted with many rich and powerful Americans, including politicians, industrialists, and philanthropists such as Andrew Carnegie, John D. Rockefeller, and Henry Huttleston Rogers of Standard Oil.

Washington was well liked by many whites, partly because of what came to be called the accommodationist view that he promoted. Accommodationism as spelled out by Washington was the idea that blacks could achieve real political and social freedom only by raising themselves economically first. Washington believed that blacks in the South would do well to first learn a trade and gradually work themselves up the economic ladder through success in business or the trades. He saw no need for higher education for most African Americans and certainly no need to agitate for political or social rights. Washington thought that whites would accept economically successful blacks.

Tuskegee students in a workshop

The accommodation part of his philosophy related to southern whites. He believed that blacks should work with or around the prejudices of whites in order to eventually receive equal rights. This philosophy was attractive to almost all white leaders, north and south, because it allowed them to agree with an African American leader while allowing segregation (strongly favored by their white constituents) to continue.

Washington had made a speech at the Atlanta Cotton States and International Exposition in 1895 that defined his viewpoint and delighted white leaders. It came to be known as the "Atlanta Compromise." Up until that speech, most African American leaders, including Ida, had praised Washington for his hard work at Tuskegee. In the speech, Washington didn't say anything that he hadn't already said about African Americans acquiring wealth and education rather than agitating for rights. But it soon became apparent that whites and blacks interpreted some of his words differently.

One phrase in his speech was quoted over and over: "In all things that are purely social we can be as separate as the fingers, yet one as the hand in all things essential to mutual progress." African Americans at that time had no desire to socialize with whites, so that didn't seem to give away anything, but whites thought that Washington was advocating segregation in public places. Segregation was not what Washington wanted, but his popularity soared among white leaders after the speech.

Ida and other black leaders had mixed feelings about Washington after the Atlanta speech, but most felt he was too conciliatory to the white community. By the end of the century, outright hostility toward Washington had begun to surface.

An April 1899 lynching in Georgia increased Ida's disenchantment with Washington. Sam Hose was tortured and burned alive after he killed his white employer, apparently in self-defense. A false rumor had circulated that he had also raped the employer's wife. Everything about the lynching was particularly horrible. The victim was not only tortured and burned, but his charred remains were sold for souvenirs in what was described as a sort of grisly picnic atmosphere. Ida immediately raised money in Chicago to send a detective to investigate the crime.

The detective's report showed that whites had lied in their accounts of the events. The report was published widely in black newspapers and a few white ones. Ida gave a speech about the report and published a pamphlet, *Lynch Law in Georgia*, to publicize the results. In this pamphlet Ida wrote: "Samuel Hose was burned, to teach the African Americans that no matter what a white man does to them, they must not resist."

Booker T. Washington failed to comment on the lynching at first. After urging from his friend, T. Thomas Fortune, Washington wrote a letter to southern newspapers. The letter said that most lynchings were not the result of rape, but he went on to say that black crime was widespread, and African Americans should do what they could to curtail any crimes against women. It was an oddly lukewarm letter that offered no reproach for the illegal killing of a man. Soon after this incident, Ida began to distance herself from Washington.

The summer of 1899 was a busy one in the Barnett household. Ida and Ferdinand were deeply involved in making arrangements for the first annual meeting of the Afro-American Council, which would be held in Chicago. Coincidentally, the National Association of Colored Women (NACW) was holding its meeting in Chicago at about the same time.

Ida was not asked to help with the organization of the NACW meeting, but she didn't notice the oversight at first because she was busy preparing for the Afro-American Council meeting. When the NACW president, Mary Terrell, arrived in Chicago, she told Ida that she had received letters from some of the Chicago club women, who stated that they would not help with the convention if Ida participated.

Ida wrote later of this action: "It was a staggering blow and all the harder to understand because it was women whom I had started in club work, and to whom I had given all the assistance in my power, who had done this thing." Nevertheless, Ida promised Terrell that she wouldn't "inflict my presence upon the organization."

Ida didn't attend the meeting, that is until the third day. She went to extend an invitation to lunch at Hull House from Jane Addams, who, by many accounts, was the most prominent woman in America at the time. Addams and a college friend had founded Hull House, the first settlement house in the U.S., in Chicago in 1889. Eventually, Hull House expanded to a thirteen-building settlement complex. Addams also was a key advocate for the passage of child-labor laws and the establishment of the nation's first juvenile court. So there was prestige in extending the lunch invitation from Addams to the clubwomen, and when Ida entered the NACW meeting her wounded feelings were soothed by the fuss that the women made over her.

In her autobiography, Ida wrote that she thought that Terrell tried to keep her away so that Ida couldn't offer competition for the

Jane Addams opened Hull House in the midst of a neighborhood populated by immigrants from all corners of the world.

In this photo from the 1920s, children line up for meals at Hull House.

presidency of the NACW. It wouldn't have been the first time that Ida's strong personality put her on the outs with other women.

The Afro-American Council meeting that followed the NACW convention was exciting for Ida. She spoke about lynching, and her husband spoke about disfranchisement. Ida had invited several women to be part of the program to encourage their support. She also invited Mary Church Terrell and Margaret Washington to a banquet at the Sherman Hotel. When she asked Booker T. Washington's wife to speak, however, she declined. Margaret Washington said that her husband had been criticized by the council the previous day.

The day before, council members had discussed the fact that Washington was not attending the sessions but did request a private meeting with the council president, Bishop Walters. Fortune had evidently advised Washington not to attend the convention because there would be no way to control the speeches and resolutions that came out of the event. Fortune feared that Washington might be embarrassed by strong resolutions against President McKinley.

Ida reported that the discussion of the issue had passed without a problem, but a newspaper reporter concocted an article saying that Washington had been criticized. There was much angry talk between Washington supporters and others when this article was published. It was the beginning of many difficulties for the council regarding Booker T. Washington.

Ida was pleased with the group's formation of an anti-lynching bureau, which she was to head. She hoped to use the bureau to expand her anti-lynching crusade. She set up an office in Chicago and mailed letters asking for contributions to fund lynching investigations. She pointed to the success of the investigation into the Sam Hose lynching and explained the bureau's purpose: "The work of that bureau is to be the same as that which I have individually conducted for the past seven years: agitating, investigating and publishing facts and figures in the lynching evil."

In spite of seven years of hard effort by Ida, lynchings still occurred with deadly regularity, and there was no federal anti-lynching law on the horizon.

# EIGHT
## *Challenging Authority*

The year 1900 was a presidential election year, and Ferdinand Barnett headed the western office of the Negro Bureau for the Republican National Committee. He had held the same job in 1896 and had proven so useful that he secured an appointment as an assistant state's attorney for Illinois.

Although women couldn't vote yet, Ida was invited to travel through Missouri making speeches on behalf of Republican candidates. Some of the black politicians in Missouri initially doubted Ida's usefulness, but they were proven wrong. She attracted big crowds in towns across Missouri, culminating with a huge rally in Kansas City.

About the same time, Ida undertook a different kind of campaign in Chicago. The *Chicago Daily Tribune* printed a series of articles that seemed to show great benefits for having a segregated school system as opposed to the mixed-race system that Chicago had. The articles quoted white parents and superintendents of segregated school systems in St. Louis, Baltimore, and other cities. There were no quotes from black parents or from heads of mixed-school systems.

Ida composed a letter to the editor of the *Chicago Daily Tribune* pointing out the faulty research of the articles and asking if the paper would allow a delegation of black citizens to visit him to express their views. She didn't receive an answer, and the letter wasn't printed. After waiting what she considered a reasonable amount of time, she went to visit Robert Patterson, editor of the paper.

They didn't get off to a very good start when Patterson mistook Ida as a black woman who had come to collect for one of the area black churches. But Ida laughed and took the advantage as they chatted about segregated schools. She soon understood that Patterson's views were distinctly southern when he informed her "that he did not believe that it was right that ignorant African Americans should have the right to vote and to rule white people because they [African Americans] were in the majority."

Ida replied with typical bluntness. "My reply to him was that I did not think it was any more fair for that type of Negro to rule than it was for that same class of white men in the First Ward flophouses who cast a ruling vote for the great First Ward of the city of Chicago." She went on to say to Patterson: "Even so, I was not disposed to condemn all white people because of that situation nor deprive the better class of them of their rights in the premises."

Ida left knowing that she was going to have to use a different approach to stop the segregation campaign for which Patterson was laying the groundwork. She promptly called Jane Addams at Hull House to request an appointment to speak to her. At that meeting, Ida explained the situation to Addams and asked: "Miss Addams, there are plenty of people in Chicago who would not sanction such a move if they knew about it. Will you undertake to reach those of influence who would be willing to do for us what we cannot do for ourselves?"

Addams agreed, and Ida subsequently spoke to a group of white editors, social service workers, ministers, and others. They were surprised to hear that the *Tribune* seemed to be backing a move toward segregated schools, and they appointed a committee to call on Patterson. Ida wrote later that she didn't know what the committee members

Jane Addams

said to the editor, but the articles ceased and there was no further call for school segregation.

The Afro-American Council met in Indianapolis in the summer of 1900. The meeting convened and the members were met with the news that Booker T. Washington had scheduled a meeting at the same time in Boston. Washington was forming a National Negro Business League. Ida observed that he seemed to have "taken a leaf out of our book to organize what would be a nonpolitical body and yet would give him the moral support that he had begun to feel he needed in his school work." Ida was referring to the fund-raising work he did among northern whites to support his Alabama school, the Tuskegee Institute.

Washington's meeting drew from prominent black citizens who might have attended the Indianapolis gathering, but Ida said that the council made the best of the situation. Washington's move further emphasized the gap he continued to reinforce between his own accommodationist views and those of many other black leaders, including Ida and W. E. B. Du Bois.

Du Bois would soon take the lead in advocating for black rights. Like Ida, Du Bois had first supported Washington. But he found that he couldn't agree with Washington's emphasis on industrial education or with Washington's stance against advocacy for black rights.

Ida's feelings about Washington, as she wrote later, mirrored those of Du Bois: "Mr. Washington's theory had been that we ought not to spend our time agitating for our rights; that we had better give attention to trying to be first class people in a jim crow car than insisting that the jim crow car should be abolished; that we should spend more time practicing industrial pursuits and getting education to fit us for this work than in going to college and striving for a college education."

W. E. B. Du Bois

Ida maintained a powerful presence in the Afro-American Council after the 1900 meeting. She kept her position as head of the Anti-Lynching Bureau and was also chosen as the national organizer. President William McKinley was reelected and then assassinated in 1901. Vice President Theodore Roosevelt took over, and soon Booker T. Washington because Roosevelt's adviser on all things related to African Americans. Washington's influence grew quickly until it seemed he could even control political appointments.

Ida had to miss the 1901 Afro-American Council meeting, held in Philadelphia, because she was about to give birth to her third child, Ida Jr. Ferdinand attended and gave Ida's report for her. She remained director of the Anti-Lynching Bureau but was replaced as the national organizer.

In 1902, Booker T. Washington attended the annual Afro-American Council meeting. Apparently, his influence had increased so much that he felt he could control the meeting's resolutions. The 1902 meeting heralded basic philosophical changes in the organization. Fortune took over as president, and most of the new officers were Bookerites, as Washington supporters were sometimes called.

Ida remained as director of the Anti-Lynching Bureau but said there were no funds for mailings or pamphlets. By 1903, it seems, Ida had withdrawn from the organization completely.

Ida focused much of her enormous energy on local and state projects. Her friendship with prominent white club member Mary Plummer led to the inclusion of black women in the founding of a federation of Cook County clubs. In early 1903, Ida spoke at the Chicago Political Equality League about African American women. She advocated friendships between black and white women as a way to overcome prejudice.

Another white woman, Celia Parker Woolley, came to Ida with an idea to start a center in which blacks and whites could meet for cultural and educational activities. The two women agreed that this might help the two races better understand each other. Ida held a meeting of her friends and solicited funds to assist in making payments on the center building. The Frederick Douglass Center opened in late 1904 with some controversy. Refreshments were served during the business meetings, and a few whites considered this to be an effort to make them accept blacks as social equals.

Controversy or not, the Douglass Center was successful, and by 1905 it offered a full schedule of activities. The center included a kindergarten, sewing classes, a young people's lyceum, a men's forum, athletic clubs for boys and girls, and more. Both Ida and Ferdinand were deeply involved with the center. Ferdinand organized the athletic clubs, and both Barnetts taught classes and gave lectures.

The Barnetts' fourth child, Alfreda, had been born in September 1904, but there's no evidence that this slowed Ida down very much. In fact, she was annoyed when Woolley seemed determined to elect a white woman as president of the newly formed Frederick Douglass Women's Club. Ida became vice president instead when no one else would serve.

Ida and Woolley soon disagreed over a program Ida arranged for the club. Asked to provide a program at the last minute, Ida put together several speakers, including herself, and she spoke on "What It Means to Be a Mother." After the speakers finished, Woolley was asked to speak. She attempted to downplay the role of motherhood by reminding the audience that many influential women were not mothers. Ida took offense, although she conceded that "all of what she said was true." After the meeting, the two women's relationship was never the same again.

Ida and Plummer, the Women's Club president, did get along and worked together on many projects, that is until the Atlanta riot occurred in September 1906.

Atlanta seemed an unlikely place for a race riot because it was often considered to be a model city of the South. Jobs were plentiful for blacks and whites, and educational and cultural opportunities were numerous. The city was home to six black colleges. But Atlanta was very segregated, and racial tensions began to flare in the summer of 1906.

M. Hoke Smith was running for Georgia governor that year on an extremely racist platform. He advocated disfranchisement for all blacks and outlined ways to do this. His campaign allowed white supremacist viewpoints to be discussed, and this led to racial tension. It appeared that Atlanta newspapers were determined to help Smith's campaign, as they printed sensationalized accounts of alleged crimes committed by black men against white women. By September, animosity between the races was at a fever pitch.

On September 22, 1906, several Atlanta newspapers printed reports of four alleged assaults on local white women by black men. It was later said that the assaults included a black man hiding in a bush, a black man looking in a window, a black man jumping out at a white woman, and a black man grabbing a woman. None of these accounts were ever verified. The newspapers featured lurid headlines that further stirred up whites.

That night, a huge mob of white men and boys surged into the black part of town attacking any black person they encountered. Later reports stated that as many as 10,000 whites may have participated in the riot, which lasted several days. Black citizens were beaten and killed, and their homes and businesses were burned. By the time the militia restored order, twenty-five black people and two whites had been killed. That was the official count, but estimates for black deaths ranged from forty to one hundred.

The Atlanta Riot was widely publicized across the nation, and soon a refugee from the riot was asked to speak to the Douglass Center's Women's Club. J. Max Barber, editor of a black magazine in Atlanta, the *Voice*, had fled to Chicago. He presented his story to the club soon after.

Ida later described Plummer's response to the harrowing tale: "Mrs. Plummer, the president said, 'I do not know what we can do or say about this terrible affair, but there is one thing I can say and that is to urge all of you to drive the criminals out from among you." Ida was appalled at such a remark and rose immediately to disagree.

Group picture from the first meeting of
the Niagara Movement in July 1905

She urged passage of a strongly worded resolution condemning the outrage in Atlanta.

Arguments began, and the resolution was not passed. Ida tried to explain her stand to Plummer, and later she wrote a letter asking that their friendship might be maintained. Ida reported Plummer's response to the letter: "Her reply showed me very clearly that I had sinned beyond redemption with her when I had dared to challenge a statement of hers in public."

Soon after this episode, Ida made a final break with the Frederick Douglass Center and with Celia Woolley. The two argued over the presidency of the Women's Club after Plummer declined to run again. Ida apparently took some pleasure in the fact that the center remained open only two more years after she left. She attributed the failure to the "loss of the woman [herself] who had labored so hard to make it a success."

Ida said that two years later, Woolley asked her to return to the center. Ida advised that she was now involved in other work, which took all of her time. Ida said she was sure that Woolley regretted her actions two years before, which had resulted in Ida's departure.

During these years, when Ida's work was done primarily in Chicago, a couple of important developments occurred on the national level. In 1905, Du Bois and radical activist Monroe Trotter had put together a meeting of like-minded black activists to start a new protest movement. They first met in Niagara Falls, New York, so the movement became known as the Niagara Movement. Both Barnetts supported the organization, but it soon faltered because of opposition from Booker T. Washington supporters. (At that time, Washington was probably at the height of his power.) The Niagara Movement's most important purpose was to pave the way for the establishment of the National Association for the Advancement of Colored People (NAACP) in 1909.

In August 1908, a race riot in Springfield, Illinois, shook the nation and proved that racial violence was not confined to the South. Black newspapers mourned the fact that the violence had taken place in the city in which Abraham Lincoln, often called the Great

Conciliator, was buried. Even liberal whites began to stir as they remembered the spirit of the abolitionists of the prior century.

Finally, a group of white progressives issued what became known as "The Call." Ida and Du Bois were among the signers of the call for a renewed struggle to obtain civil rights for the black race. Symbolically, "The Call" was issued on the hundredth anniversary of Lincoln's birth in February 1909.

The National Negro Conference convened in New York City on May 31, 1909. Some three hundred people attended, among them prominent scientists, scholars, and activists. There were three black speakers: Ida, Du Bois, and Bishop Walters. Ida spoke about lynching and finished by proposing federal anti-lynching legislation and a bureau to investigate and publish the details of each lynching.

By the second day of the conference, much of the goodwill between black and white leaders seemed a little frayed. They argued over resolutions to be offered and over who should be on a committee to plan a permanent organization. In a late-night committee session, Ida's name was first put on the list and then removed. Ida had seen the list and knew that she was to be included, so she was stunned the next morning when her name was not on the "Committee of Forty."

After the session adjourned, Ida walked outside in an uproar. Friends called her back, and Du Bois told her that he had removed her name. Du Bois had replaced her with C. E. Bentley, an Illinois member of the Niagara Movement. He offered to add her back to the list, but she refused. "I did a foolish thing," Ida wrote later. "My anger at having been treated in such fashion outweighed my judgment and I again left the building." She regretted her decision because she felt she ought to have been more supportive of the group as a whole. Eventually, Ida's name was added to the list by the committee chairman, Charles Edward Russell, and she participated for several years.

An event in Cairo, Illinois, in November 1909 and Ida's response to it did much to raise her standing among other black leaders. A state anti-lynching law had been passed in Illinois in 1905. It required "the governor to remove from office forthwith the sheriff of any county in which a man, black or white, has been taken by force from jail or the custody of that sheriff and lynched." The sheriff could file for reinstatement, and the governor could reinstate the law enforcement officer, if it was found that the sheriff had done all in his power to protect the life of the prisoner.

A young white woman had been found strangled in Cairo, Illinois, and a local black man, William "Frog" James, a coal driver, had been arrested on circumstantial evidence. Sheriff Frank Davis said that, fearing a lynching, he and a deputy took James from the jail and out into the woods. The mob found them and hung James. Afterward, they shot the body hundreds of times, burned it, and put the man's head on a fencepost.

Spectators cram Commercial Avenue in Cairo, Illinois, on November 11, 1909, to view the lynching of William James.

Ida wrote later of how the incident had affected her household. Ferdinand had come home to say that he couldn't persuade anyone to go to Cairo and investigate the crime. News had come back to Chicago that Sheriff Davis might have cooperated with the mob by signaling his position in the woods to them so they could capture James. Ferdinand wanted Ida to travel to Cairo and investigate.

Ida had been criticized before for doing what should have been men's work. It wasn't convenient for her to go, and she told her husband at the dinner table that she didn't want to do it. She said that "for once I was quite willing to let them attend to the job," meaning the men of her race. She rose from the table and took her youngest daughter upstairs to sing her to sleep. Ferdinand turned back to his newspaper, and Ida thought that was the end of it.

A little while later, after Ida had fallen asleep by Alfreda, her oldest son Charles shook her shoulder. Ida related their conversation in her autobiography: "I was awakened by my oldest child, who said, 'Mother, Pa says it is time to go.' 'Go where?' I said, 'I told your father downstairs that I was not going. I don't see why I should have to go and do the work that the others refuse.' My boy was only ten years old. He and the other children had been present at the dinner table when their father told the story. He stood by the bedside a little while and then said, 'Mother if you don't go nobody else will.'"

Charles's plea to his mother did the job. The whole family took Ida to the train in the morning. She said of her children that day, "They were intensely interested and for the first time were willing to see me leave home." Ida waved good-bye and turned her attention to the hard job that awaited her in Cairo.

# NINE
## *Making a Difference in Illinois*

When Ida arrived in Cairo that evening, she sought out the local A.M.E. minister for advice. The pastor told her that the general opinion of blacks in town was that William James was a worthless sort, and most people thought he had probably done the crime he was lynched for. Ida saw right away that this wouldn't be an easy case to investigate. She wasted no time in telling the minister that he and other African Americans shouldn't be allowing the lynching of one of their race to go unchallenged. He directed her to Will Taylor, who was a druggist in town. Ida discovered that she had known Taylor when he lived in Chicago.

Taylor was cooperative and arranged a place for Ida to stay, then took her around the next day to speak to various black citizens. She organized a mass meeting for that night, which was well attended. Ida asked them plainly if anyone knew if Sheriff Frank Davis had locked up James and protected him from the mob. Most of the crowd liked Sheriff Davis because he had treated blacks fairly and had some black deputies. But even so, they couldn't say that he had done all he could to protect his prisoner.

The group agreed to write a resolution to that effect, and Ida left Cairo the next morning with that resolution and a second one, which she had received from a group of Baptist ministers who were meeting in town. She arrived at the state capitol on the morning of a scheduled hearing before the governor, which would determine whether or not Sheriff Davis—who had been suspended—would be reinstated. Ferdinand had sent a legal brief for Ida to pick up at the post office.

Ida was surprised to discover that she was the only black person in the hearing room. She shared the room with white lawyers and priests and other representatives who had traveled to Springfield to offer support to Sheriff Davis. Petitions and other evidence were presented on behalf of the sheriff. Nearly five hundred African American men had signed petitions that had been circulated at barbershops in Cairo. Ida had heard of these petitions while she was in Cairo and had gone to some of the barbershops in question. She recalled that "to the few [customers] who happened to be standing around I gave the most blistering talk that I could lay my tongue to."

When all of the testimony for Davis was finished, Governor Charles Deneen turned to Ida and said that he understood she was there to represent the colored people of Illinois. Ida said later: "Not until that moment did I realize that the burden depended upon me." At this point an acquaintance of Ida's, who had stopped by the capitol only to invite Ida to dinner, stepped up to her side and remained there throughout her testimony. He was a lawyer, and Ida was thankful for his help since she was unfamiliar with legal procedure in a courtroom.

Ida read the brief that Ferdinand had sent and added the facts she had discovered in her investigation. She told the circumstances of the resolutions signed at the mass meeting and at the ministers' meeting. In conclusion, she said: "Governor, the state of Illinois has had too many terrible lynchings within her borders within the last few years. If this man is sent back it will be an encouragement to those who resort to mob violence and will do so at any time, well knowing that they will not be called to account for doing so."

The two sides got together to write what they called an agreed statement of facts, which described the circumstances of the lynching in Cairo. Ida argued with the state's attorney and with the sheriff's lawyers over the wording, but finally a document was submitted to Governor Deneen for his decision. Ida didn't think there was much chance that the sheriff would be refused reinstatement because there was so much pressure from every direction. She told the lawyer friend who helped her: "We have done the best we could under the circumstances, and angels could do no more."

The following week, Governor Deneen issued a proclamation stating that Sheriff Davis would not be reinstated because he had not properly protected his prisoner as required by Illinois state law. The *Chicago Defender* newspaper gave tribute to Ida's triumph: "If we only had a few men with the backbone of Mrs. Barnett, lynching would soon come to a halt in America."

There were no more lynchings in Illinois. An attempted lynching in Cairo the next year ended when the new sheriff fired at the mob and killed a prominent white Cairo citizen. Ida's work on the James case probably had a bigger direct effect on lynching in Illinois than any work she had done before.

After the Cairo episode, Ida received a special invitation from the Committee of Forty to attend a meeting on May 25, 1910. John Milholland, one of the white committee members who had vigorously supported her, wrote in a letter "that the committee regarded that [the Cairo incident] as the most outstanding thing that had been done for the race during the year."

It was at this meeting that the organization received its permanent name, the National Association for

> "If we only had a few men with the backbone of Mrs. Barnett, lynching would soon come to a halt in America."
>
> The *Chicago Defender*

the Advancement of Colored People. Ida was named a member of the executive committee, and it was at this meeting that the organization agreed to launch a journal called *The Crisis*. Du Bois was appointed to edit the new journal. This meeting was the high point of Ida's participation in the NAACP, although she remained active for several years.

During the summer of 1910, Ida was persuaded to attend a meeting of the National Association of Colored Women. She hadn't been active in the group since 1899, but the current NACW president, Elizabeth Carter, wanted Ida to attend the Louisville meeting that summer and speak about the NAACP. Ida was also appointed head of the resolutions committee and was greeted warmly by the delegates. But she had brought controversy with her.

Ida supported a move to change the way the organization's publication, the *National Notes*, was edited and published. For ten years, the

A 1902 photo of a reading room at Tuskegee Institute

*Notes* had been edited by Margaret Washington (Booker T. Washington's wife) and printed by Tuskegee Institute students at no cost to the NACW. Evidently, there had been complaints about the newsletter's content being biased toward Washington as well as concerns about poor delivery. But since it was printed free, nothing had been done to change the situation.

The NACW executive committee chairman, Ione Gibbs, presented a report recommending that the editor of the *National Notes* be elected and that the publication be under the organization's direct control.

Ida congratulated Gibbs on her report and recommended a yes vote. After discussion, Ida called for a vote and the motion passed, but the president ruled that the motion was out of order. There was an appeal, and the delegates grew heated in their responses. Ida was hissed at by some of the women for her part in the disagreement. She recalled: "I went home and went to bed instead of appearing at the big banquet which was given to the delegates that night."

Ida insisted in her autobiography that her only motive was to help resolve the issues with the *National Notes* that the women themselves hadn't been able to address. It's just as likely that Ida saw this resolution as a way to rid the NACW of the influence of Booker T. Washington.

Ida's problems with national organizations continued when the NAACP duplicated her efforts in a lynching case and then failed to acknowledge her efforts. Steve Green, a black Arkansas farmer, had shot his employer in self-defense and then fled north to Chicago. Once there, he was betrayed and sent by train back south. Ida organized a rescue and eventually got Green to Canada. The NAACP belatedly sent money and then failed to mention her part when the event was described in *The Crisis*.

Ida was busy on the local scene in 1910, and that involvement probably yielded a great deal more satisfaction for her than her activities with national movements. She had begun teaching a Sunday school class for young black men at Grace Presbyterian Church in Chicago. Around the time of the Springfield, Illinois, riot, some of the young men began meeting at the Barnetts' home on Sunday afternoons to discuss the issues surrounding that riot and other racial incidents. The group named itself the Negro Fellowship League.

Ida's work with the Cairo lynching and the Steve Green case inspired the league to become an activist group rather than just a discussion society. Ida felt strongly that young black men in Chicago had nowhere to get together socially except the saloon, and that led to crime and arrest. She spent considerable time visiting young black prisoners in the Joliet, Illinois, prison to hear their stories. She found that some of them were educated and had come from good homes. The similarities between their stories were that they had come to Chicago without knowing anyone and had gotten into trouble on State Street, which Ida called the "Great White Way" of Chicago because of its saloons, gambling houses, and poolrooms.

Ida and the other league members wanted to start some sort of mission or settlement house on State Street, but there was no money for such an undertaking. After the members agreed that they would like to do something to help other African Americans, Ida was invited to speak about lynching at a dinner given by the Congregational Union. One of the other speakers gave statistics about the higher crime rate among blacks in Chicago. Ida was asked to dispute that statement, but she replied that she could not because it was true.

After giving her talk about lynching, Ida gave her views on the cause of the higher crime rate for blacks. She said: "All other races in the city are welcomed into the settlements, YMCAs, YWCAs, gymnasiums, and every other movement for uplift if only their skins are white. Only one social center welcomes the Negro, and that is the saloon. Ought we to wonder at the harvest which we have heard enumerated tonight?"

After the meeting, a woman asked Ida if it was a fact that the YMCAs did not admit black men. At Ida's affirmative answer, the women said she was sure her husband didn't know that, and he had given several thousand dollars to the YMCA in the last year.

A few months later, this woman telephoned Ida to arrange a meeting to talk about the problem with the YMCA. The woman turned out to be Jessie Lawson, whose husband was the owner and publisher of the *Chicago Daily News*. Jessie Lawson was prepared to help Ida and the league finance a center on State Street.

With the Lawsons' financial help, the Negro Fellowship League Reading Room and Social Center opened its doors at 2830 State Street on May 1, 1910. One paid staff member and a group of volunteers ran the center. Young men dropped in to read, socialize, play checkers, and so on from 9:00 a.m. to 10:00 p.m., and soon the upstairs was turned into a men's lodging house. An employment bureau evolved as employers stopped by to look for likely workers among the young men gathered at the center. Eventually, the city required a business license for the employment bureau because it was placing so many people in jobs. The center absorbed much of Ida's energy for the ten years it was in existence.

In 1911, Ida returned to journalism by starting a newspaper, the *Fellowship Herald*, and she was invited to join the Colored Press Association of Chicago in 1912.

In 1913, Victor Lawson shifted his funding from the league's center to a new branch of the YMCA, which had opened in the black district. Ida supported the new YMCA but felt that it didn't serve all of the same purposes as the Negro Fellowship League Center did. Moreover, the YMCA charged twelve dollars a year to join. This fee would be beyond the reach of many young black men. The center was forced to move to smaller quarters without the lodging rooms, and Ida took a full-time job to help pay the center's expenses.

In late May 1913, Ida began work as Chicago's first black adult probation officer. She was allowed to meet her probationers at the league center so she could still oversee the operations there. Her workload grew heavy, and she lobbied for more black probation officers.

In 1915, her contract was not renewed, probably because of her lobbying and because she had supported the losing candidate for Chicago mayor that year. Ida was able to keep the center running for five more years even without her salary.

Ida had long been interested in women's suffrage, and when the suffrage movement picked up steam, Ida formed a black women's suffrage group. The Alpha Suffrage Club (ASC) first met in January 1913. One of the group's first official acts was to send Ida to Washington, D.C., as its delegate to a national suffrage parade. It was being held on March 3, 1913, in connection with Woodrow Wilson's presidential inauguration.

Yet again, Ida found herself embroiled in controversy. Southern white women refused to march in the same delegations as black women, whom they felt should march in a blacks-only delegation. The organizer wanted to go along with the demand even though she personally didn't agree with the exclusion.

Ida told the *Chicago Daily Tribune*: "The southern women have tried to evade the question time and time again by giving some excuse or other every time it has been brought up. If the Illinois women do not take a stand now in this great democratic parade then the colored women are lost." She added an ultimatum: "I shall not march at all unless I can march under the Illinois banner."

A compromise apparently was reached when two white delegates from Illinois said they were going to march in the colored section with Ida. But when the parade started, the two women took their places in the regular Illinois delegation. Soon after, Ida slipped from the sidelines to march beside the other Illinois delegates without the leader's knowledge.

Ida was quite active in local and state efforts to gain the vote for women. The Alpha Suffrage Club campaigned door-to-door in 1913 to get women to register to vote after a limited suffrage bill was passed in Illinois that year. The Presidential and Municipal Suffrage Bill granted women presidential and municipal but not state suffrage. More than

Suffragettes marching in the early 1900s

153,000 black and white Chicago women registered on the first day they were eligible.

In 1913, the Barnetts had joined Monroe Trotter's National Equal Rights League (NERL). The organization, which had existed in some form since 1908, was a vehicle for Trotter's viewpoints, which generally were in opposition to the NAACP's. Trotter was perhaps the most militant of all activists of that time. He had founded the radical newspaper *Boston Guardian* in 1901 and had helped start the Niagara Movement in 1905. He formed the NERL after concluding that the NAACP was too moderate for his support.

By 1915, Ida and Ferdinand had also given up on the NAACP and directed all their protest efforts through the NERL. Ida collaborated with Trotter on many protest activities. The two both disliked the compromising ways of the NAACP. For the most part, Ida combined the activities of the Negro Fellowship League and the Chicago branch of the NERL. Also in 1913, Ida—with the help of the NERL—led a successful fight to keep Illinois from passing a law that would segregate public transportation. The combined forces also fought against congressional bills that would have forbidden interracial marriage in the District of Columbia.

These years were extremely busy ones for Ida, but she still maintained a home and looked after her children. She visited their schools and kept track of their social activities. Ferdinand often worked at home, so when Ida was also working there on her multiple projects, the household was full of people and activities. The children met many famous people, and also came in contact with some of the many clients their father represented for free. Ferdinand did the cooking, and the cleaning was done by someone other than Ida, for she hated the repetitive nature of household tasks. But she knew how to manage a household, and she made sure that her children were taught the same skills. It was a happy time for the Barnett family.

# TEN
## *Final Crusades*

When World War I began in Europe in 1914, Americans soon felt the results even though the country would not enter the war until 1917. The war influenced black and white relationships in profound ways, as economic demands produced new opportunities for African Americans. European immigration had slowed to a trickle as the war spread over the continent. This meant fewer workers coming to the U.S. to fill the increasing number of jobs being created by booming industrialization. This increasing industrialization was present before the war, but it shifted into high gear to meet the needs of the military.

At the same time, the boll weevil—a beetle that feeds on flowers and cotton buds—was completing its march across the southern cotton-growing plantations. First seen in the U.S. around 1892, the boll weevil moved across acres of cotton in a steady path north and east. The cotton industry was almost destroyed by 1915. This left thousands of black cotton workers and tenant farmers without work. They streamed north to such urban areas as St. Louis and Chicago.

Black troops stand in formation in this 1917 photo. After fighting for freedom in Europe, many felt they deserved the same freedoms at home.

This movement, which became known as the "Great Migration," disturbed the status quo of black-white relations in the North. African Americans had been largely banned from factory jobs until this time, but the increased demand for workers began to change this. Factory owners and managers were less concerned about the race of their workers than they were about filling jobs so that production could expand. White factory workers and prospective new workers were not so understanding of management's needs.

Racial tensions rose dramatically in such places as East St. Louis, Illinois, due to economic competition between white residents and the migrating African Americans. A race riot was sparked in East St. Louis on July 2, 1917, by tension over job security at two of the city's manufacturing plants. Early reports reached Ida in Chicago the next morning. Officially, the number of dead was listed at thirty-nine blacks and nine whites, but news reports said as many as one hundred black men, women, and children died from beatings, fires, and shootings.

Ida called a protest meeting that evening, and the attendees adopted resolutions to send to Illinois governor Frank Lowden calling for a complete investigation. The group also took up a collection to send Ida to East St. Louis so that she could determine what had happened. She arrived in the city on July 5. Ida quickly found that law enforcement officials had done almost nothing to stop the rioting and, in fact, may had taken part in the looting and vandalism that destroyed hundreds of black homes.

Back in Chicago, Ida published a pamphlet about the riot. She traveled to Springfield to urge the governor to investigate and to provide relief funds for the displaced blacks. Money was not available for relief, Lowden said, but both state and federal investigations began. Arrests were made, but it soon became apparent that blacks were receiving much more severe sentences for their alleged crimes than were the whites who had participated in arson, shootings, and beatings.

Ida was asked to further investigate the case of Leroy Bundy, a black dentist in East St. Louis, who appeared to have become a scapegoat for the riot. He was accused of encouraging blacks to arm themselves, and he was consequently charged with the murder of two policemen who had been killed during the riot. The NAACP had agreed to provide counsel for Bundy, but when Ida visited the man in jail, he said that he had not been contacted. Eventually, Ida and Ferdinand were able to win Bundy's freedom, but it took years of trials and appeals. Their crusade undermined their relationship with NAACP leaders, who said they had matters in hand for Bundy even though there was no evidence to support that view when Ida first saw Bundy.

In August 1917, yet another riot erupted. An African American army battalion had been sent to Houston in late July. The soldiers found that they were very unwelcome in this southern city and soon were targeted for their refusal to abide by Houston customs concerning segregation. On August 23, a riot broke out and twenty people died. Courts martial for murder followed, and thirteen hastily convicted

Ida B. Wells-Barnett wearing the lapel button

African Americans were hanged on December 11, 1917, after being denied the right of appeal.

Ida and many other African Americans viewed the soldiers as martyrs. She tried to organize a memorial service in Chicago, but no churches would allow her to use their facilities. She settled for distributing lapel buttons that said "In Memorial MARTYRED NEGRO SOLDIERS."

The buttons attracted the attention of authorities, who told her that she was committing treason by promoting the sentiment on the buttons. The U.S. had entered the war the prior spring, and government officials, including lawmakers, had become almost paranoid about behavior that implied disloyalty to the U.S. or its war aims. Ida was supportive of the war and told the two Secret Service men who came to interview her that fact. She even showed them the tables of candy, cigarettes, and other gifts that she was preparing to send to Fort Grant for black soldiers.

The gentlemen insisted that she must give them the buttons in order to escape arrest. They also told her that most blacks didn't agree with her stand about the Houston soldiers. She replied that perhaps they didn't know any better. As for herself, she said: "I would consider it an honor to spend whatever years are necessary in prison as the one member of the race who protested." The Secret Service men seemed taken aback and left without the buttons, never to come back.

By 1919 the war had ended, and discharged soldiers flooded back into the labor market. This created more racial tension, as blacks who had fought for their country's freedom thought that they should be allowed equal chances at employment. The middle months of that year would become known as the Red Summer of 1919 because of the blood that was shed in racial outbreaks and riots across the U.S.

Ida was personally involved in two of these incidents. The first happened in her hometown. The great black influx into Chicago before and during the war had created overcrowding on the South Side, which was populated mostly by African Americans. Middle-class blacks tried to move into previously all-white neighborhoods to escape. This caused hostility and the creation of "protective organizations" among whites to "protect" their neighborhoods. Violence followed. Ida was worried about the race situation in Chicago and twice visited the mayor's office to discuss the problems, although she was refused admittance.

On July 29, 1919, a group of black youths strayed near the white section of a swimming area at Lake Michigan in Chicago. The boys weren't strong swimmers, but they stayed near a large raft that they had built and pushed along with them. While they played in the water, a young white man walked to the end of the breakwater about seventy-five feet away. He began throwing rocks at the boys, who ducked underwater as each chunk flew toward them. They later said that they thought they were playing a game with the man. As long as they watched the hurler, he couldn't hit them from such a distance. Disaster struck when one of the boys, Eugene Williams, was distracted and forgot to watch for the rocks. Williams was hit in the forehead. The other boys tried to help but then ran to get a lifeguard. It was too late; Eugene had drowned.

Confusion reigned as police and swimmers, black and white, arrived. The white man had fled. Witnesses tried to get police to arrest him after he was identified at the nearby white swimming area. After a loud confrontation between spectators, the police arrested a black man.

This led to more fights between mobs and other groups. A rumor quickly spread that a white policeman had kept expert swimmers from saving Williams. A black man shot into a crowd and injured two policemen, who then shot the man dead. Other people pulled out revolvers and fired. For five days after this a race war raged, and sporadic violence occurred for another week.

It wasn't only whites doing the rioting, although most of it occurred in their neighborhoods. Those of both races circulated throughout the city, assaulting and beating anyone of the opposite race that they could find. Newspapers, both black and white, printed inflammatory reports, many of which were fabricated.

Ida joined with others to form the Protective Association to press for protection for her people and to insist on a thorough investigation. As the authorities struggled to gain control, whites fired on African American homes while blacks fired back from hiding. Black homes and businesses were burned as whites sought to prevent what they feared was going to be an armed black uprising.

The riot ended only when the Illinois state militia was called in to restore order and a cooling rain dampened passions. The riot left twenty-three blacks and fifteen whites dead. Hundreds were injured, and at least a thousand black family members were left homeless. Ida resigned from the Protective Association after its leaders proposed that the state attorney general, Edward Brundage, take charge of the investigation. Ida felt that Brundage had done a dismal job of investigating the East St. Louis Riot. She blamed him for the scarcity of whites who were brought to justice in that investigation.

SPRINGFIELD (ILLS.) RIOTS—MILITIA CAMP IN STATE HOUSE GROUNDS   #53-8

The Illinois state militia camped on the
state house lawn in Springfield during the riots

Ida placed her membership card on the table in protest and walked out of the meeting, only to hear someone say "good riddance" as she passed. She wrote later of her feelings: "I walked down South Parkway with tears streaming down my face, thinking of those so-called representative Negroes asking that man to do to us what he had already done in East Saint Louis. . . . I never went back to a meeting of the so-called Protective Association, and very soon it became a thing of the past."

Ida had always taken criticism personally, and this occasion was a further example of her inclination to think that she was always right and to take action upon that conviction. The atmosphere surrounding race relations had changed in the thirty or so years that Ida had been an active advocate. The NAACP and other organizations sometimes employed compromise. And compromise was not a word that Ida ever used. Her unshakable faith that she was on the side of right did not make her easy to get along with, particularly within an organization. She quit most groups eventually, even the ones she had founded, which left her feeling isolated from her cause and her people.

Ida didn't have long to stew over what she saw as the rejection of her ideas by the Protective Society. On September 30, 1919, a labor disagreement between sharecroppers and white landowners in Phillips County, Arkansas, flared into violence. Black sharecroppers had met at a church to talk about unionizing to obtain better prices from white plantation owners for the cotton the tenant farmers grew. As often happens, stories conflicted over who fired the first shot, but four days of rioting left five whites and an unknown number of blacks dead. Estimates of black fatalities ranged into the hundreds in what became known as the Elaine (Arkansas) Race Riot.

The whites of the area insisted that the African Americans were preparing to kill all the whites and take over their land. This hysteria persisted until almost three hundred black men were taken to the county jail. The county grand jury met and charged 122 blacks with crimes ranging from murder to night-riding. The first twelve men to be tried were quickly convicted and given the death penalty.

Meanwhile, Ida had taken up the cause. She spearheaded a petition drive to send notice to the Arkansas governor that organizations in Chicago would urge African Americans to leave Arkansas if the twelve men were executed. She traveled to Arkansas to investigate. She posed as a relative and visited the condemned men in jail, where they told her their stories.

The men seemed resigned to their impending executions as they talked and even sang for Ida and the prison warden who happened by. They held a type of church service as they prayed and sang about dying. Ida enjoyed the singing but not their talk of dying. She told them: "Quit talking about dying; if you believe your God is all powerful, believe he is powerful enough to open these prison doors, and say so. Dying is the last thing you ought to even think about, much less talk about. Pray to live and believe you are going to get out."

Ida went home to Chicago, where she published the condemned men's stories in a pamphlet and organized support. The Elaine rioters were taken up as a cause around the country, and eventually all twelve were released. Again Ida tangled with the NAACP, as the organization claimed credit for the men's release because of the work they had done on their behalf. Ida's inability to work with the NAACP leaders meant that much of her investigation was duplicated by that organization.

The following year was a difficult one for Ida, as she struggled to keep the Negro Fellowship League running. Finances were tight because she had lost her probation officer job, and many of the social programs the league sponsored were being offered by other organizations. The Urban League had been introduced to Chicago in 1915, and the new YMCA took away some of Ida's clientele. The larger organizations were more efficient and had financial reserves to support their work.

The twelve Elaine massacre defendants

In 1920, Ida made numerous speeches and trips on behalf of political, civic, and church causes. She taught an adult Sunday school class at a new church and was active in the Metropolitan Center Lyceum. But near the end of her hectic year, it was apparent that the Negro Fellowship League Social Center would have to close. Soon after

Thanksgiving, Ida moved out the remaining books and furniture and turned the keys over to the landlord. The closing of the league was a blow to her. She later wrote: "Although I had given ten years to the work, I had been unable to get the city, the church, or the moral forces to help us administer the 'ounce of prevention' to keep black boys from going wrong."

A week later, Ida was admitted to a local hospital for gall bladder surgery. Ida was hospitalized for five weeks. After going home, she suffered a relapse and was confined to her home for another eight weeks. Her observations about that time reveal bitterness but the same determination she had always displayed. She wrote:

> It took me a year to recover, and during that year I did more serious thinking from a personal point of view than ever before in my life. All at once the realization came to me that I had nothing to show for all those years of toil and labor. It seemed to me that I should now begin to make some preparation of a personal nature for the future, and this I set out to accomplish.

Most of her time in 1921 was spent at home. Herman's wife had given birth to Ida's first grandson, and Ida spent many happy hours with the newcomer.

By the time 1922 arrived, Ida was ready to resume her busy life of speeches, fund-raisers, and other activities on behalf of various causes. She lobbied both Congress and President Warren G. Harding in 1922 on behalf of the Dyer anti-lynching bill. Ida's connection with the anti-lynching forces had diminished significantly by this time. The NAACP was fighting hard, without Ida, to get a federal anti-lynching bill passed into law. It was mainly their efforts that got the bill to the Senate floor. The bill wasn't passed, but the crusade continued amid increased publicity by the NAACP.

Ida remained active in local Chicago clubs, including the Ida B. Wells Club. She represented the club at the national NACW meeting in Chicago in 1924. She ran for president of that organization once again, but she was defeated by a distinguished black educator, Mary McLeod Bethune.

Ida founded and worked for several local groups, such as the Women's Forum and the Third Ward Women's Political Club. She also participated in interracial organizations, including the Anthropological Society. Ida, who still knew how to stir up an audience, did so in 1926 when she presented a program on mixed marriage to the Anthropological Society. She claimed that laws against intermarriage were powerless to keep people apart. The atmosphere in the room grew tense when Ida addressed that biggest of taboos among whites.

During the presidential election campaign in 1928, Ida was appointed national organizer of the Illinois Colored Women. She plunged quickly into organizing a rally and sending out a mass mailing. But the Republican headquarters refused to pay her printing bills or pay for her to travel and speak throughout the state. It's not clear why the headquarters wouldn't pay for what appears to have been legitimate expenses. Ida paid for the printing herself and got a backer to pay the rental fee for the hall where the rally was held on September 20, 1928.

In 1930, Ida decided to run for the Illinois Senate. She was unable to get support from either of the two main Republican political factions, but she campaigned relentlessly from January 1930 until the April primary, when she received only 585 votes. It was a blow to Ida, but she rebounded to write, protest, and organize on behalf of a number of causes in 1930 and early 1931.

Ida also continued to work on her autobiography, which she had begun after a young woman at a YWCA meeting asked her about her connection to the anti-lynching movement. In the preface to her autobiography, Ida told of her encounter with the young woman and how it affected her. She wrote of her desire to record the facts of African American history and her contribution. She ended by saying: "Because our youth are entitled to the facts of race history which only the participants can give, I am thus led to set forth the facts contained in this volume which I dedicate to them."

In her book, Ida wrote about her experiences up to 1927, but ill health prevented her from continuing. After shopping on March 21, 1931, she didn't feel well that evening. She spent the next day, Sunday, in bed. By Monday, it was obvious that Ida was very ill, and she was rushed to Dailey Hospital. She was diagnosed with uremic poisoning and died on March 25.

Ida's funeral service was simple, without long speeches or testimonials. The church was packed, and the sidewalks outside were lined with people

Ida with her four children

who came to file past her coffin. The *Chicago Defender* wrote of her service: "no fanfare of trumpets, no undue shouting, no flowery oratory—just plain, earnest, sincere words from the mouths of those to whom the grief was real."

Ida's youngest daughter, Alfreda, refused to let her mother's contribution to racial justice go unnoticed by future generations. It took almost forty years, but Alfreda finally got her mother's autobiography published in 1970, with the final chapter titled "Eternal Vigilance is the Price of Liberty." In 2005, nearly seventy-five years after Ida's death, the U.S. Senate apologized for spending decades blocking some two hundred anti-lynching bills from becoming law. There to witness the Senate apology was one of Ida's grandsons.

# TIMELINE

| | |
|---|---|
| 1862 | Born a slave in Holly Springs, Mississippi, on July 16. |
| 1863 | Emancipated after President Lincoln issues the Emancipation Proclamation. |
| 1878 | Father, mother, and baby brother die in a yellow fever epidemic; becomes a teacher. |
| 1880 | Moves to Memphis with her sisters. |
| 1884 | Sues the railroad; writes her first article for the *Living Way*. |
| 1889 | Becomes co-owner of the *Free Speech*. |
| 1891 | Loses her teaching job; becomes a full-time journalist. |
| 1892 | Friend Thomas Moss is lynched in Memphis; moves to New York City. |
| 1893 | Tours England; works at the Columbian Exposition. |
| 1894 | Makes her second speaking tour in England; tours the United States. |
| 1895 | Marries Ferdinand Barnett. |
| 1896 | Son Charles is born; helps found the National Association of Colored Women. |
| 1897 | Son Herman is born. |
| 1898 | Lobbies in Washington, D.C.; the National Afro-American League is revived and renamed the Afro-American Council. |
| 1899 | Appointed head of the Afro-American Council's Anti-Lynching Bureau. |
| 1901 | Daughter Ida Jr. is born. |
| 1904 | Helps establish the Frederick Douglass Center in Chicago; daughter Alfreda is born. |
| 1909 | Becomes a founding member of the NAACP; investigates a lynching in Cairo, Illinois. |
| 1910 | Opens the Negro Fellowship League Reading Room and Social Center. |
| 1913 | Becomes Chicago's first black adult probation officer; marches in a national suffrage parade in March. |
| 1917 | Investigates the East St. Louis riot. |
| 1919 | Investigates a riot in Arkansas. |
| 1920 | Undergoes gall bladder surgery. |
| 1928 | Appointed the national organizer for the Illinois Colored Women. |
| 1930 | Runs for state senate. |
| 1931 | Dies of uremic poisoning on March 25. |

# SOURCES

## CHAPTER ONE: *A Slave's Daughter*

p. 10,      "He tried to drag me . . ." Alfreda M. Duster, ed., *Crusade for Justice: The Autobiography of Ida B. Wells* (Chicago and London: The University of Chicago Press, 1970), 18.

p. 10,      "They were encouraged . . ." Ibid., 19.

p. 16,      "I knew dimly . . ." Ibid., 9.

## CHAPTER TWO: *Teacher Ida*

p. 18,      "Jim and Lizzie Wells . . ." Duster, *Crusade for Justice*, 11.

p. 20,      "When all this had . . ." Ibid., 16.

p. 24,      "my darkest days . . ." Miriam Decosta-Willis, *The Memphis Diary of Ida B. Wells* (Boston: Beacon Press, 1995), 24.

p. 24,      "tempestuous, rebellious . . ." Ibid., 78.

p. 25,      "bought off by . . ." Duster, *Crusade for Justice*,19.

p. 26,      "I can see to this day . . ." Ibid.

p. 26,      "I felt so disappointed . . ." Decosta-Willis, *The Memphis Diary of Ida B. Wells*, 140-41.

p. 26,      "I never cared for . . ." Duster, *Crusade for Justice*, 31.

p. 28,      "Looking back at . . ." Decosta-Willis, *The Memphis Diary of Ida B. Wells*, 26.

## CHAPTER THREE: *A New Calling*

p. 32,      "I breathed freer . . ." Decosta-Willis, *The Memphis Diary of Ida B. Wells*, 113.

p.p. 32-33  "He wanted me . . ." Duster, *Crusade for Justice*, 31-32.

p. 33,      "In every way . . ." Ibid., 32.

p. 33,      "I went to Louisville . . ." Ibid.

p. 34,      "With his long . . ." Decosta-Willis, *The Memphis Diary of Ida B. Wells*, 52.

p. 34,      "If Iola were a . . ." Linda O. McMurry, *To Keep the Waters Troubled: The Life of Ida B. Wells* (New York and Oxford: Oxford University Press, 1998), 111.

p. 39,      "Mr. Montgomery came to . . ." Duster, *Crusade for Justice*, 38-39.

p. 39,      "It had been charged . . ." Ibid., 36.

p.p. 39-40, "Of course I had . . ." Ibid., 37.

p. 40,      "But I thought . . ." Ibid.

## CHAPTER FOUR: *Lynching at the Curve*

p. 44,      "tell my people . . ." Duster, *Crusade for Justice*, 51.

p. 45,      "He and his wife . . ." Ibid., 47-48.

p.p. 45-46, "There is therefore . . ." Ibid., 52.

p. 46,      "A finer, cleaner . . ." Ibid., 55.

p. 48,      "Like many another . . ." Ibid., 64.

p. 48,      "Eight Negroes lynched . . ." Ibid., 65-66.

p. 49,      "Well, we've been . . ." Ibid., 61.

CHAPTER FIVE: *England to Chicago*
p. 51,          "she has continued . . ." McMurry, *To Keep the Waters Troubled*, 154.
p. 52,          "About two months . . ." Duster, *Crusade for Justice*, 78.
p. 52,          "But this was the first . . ." Ibid., 79.
p. 52,          "every detail of . . ." Ibid.
p. 53,          "A panic seized me . . ." Ibid.
p. 53,          "the women didn't . . ." Ibid., 80.
p. 53,          "Let me give . . ." Jacqueline Jones Royster, ed., *Southern Horrors and Other Writings; The Anti-Lynching Campaign of Ida B. Wells*, 1892-1900 (Boston and New York: Bedford/St. Martins, 1997), 51.
p. 53,          "It is with no . . ." Ibid., 50.
p. 55,          "the case of the . . ." Ibid., 60.
p. 55,          "Governor Tillman . . ." Ibid., 58.
p. 56,          "The fire lighted . . ." Duster, *Crusade for Justice*, 85.
p.p. 56-57,     "she had learned . . ." Ibid.
p. 57,          "It seemed like . . ." Ibid., 86.
p. 58,          "Ida Wells is continuing . . ." McMurry, *To Keep the Waters Troubled*, 195.
p. 58,          "the negro adventuress . . ." Ibid.
p. 61,          "went straight out . . ." Duster, *Crusade for Justice*, 119.

CHAPTER SIX: *Travels for the Cause*
p. 64,          "Will you oblige me . . ." Paula J. Giddings, *Ida: A Sword Among Lions* (New York: HarperCollins, 2008), 293.
p. 64,          "I have never . . ." McMurry, *To Keep the Waters Troubled*, 208.
p. 65,          "disreputable colored . . ." Ibid., 214.
p. 65,          "are very coarse . . ." Ibid., 215.
p. 66,          "However revolting these . . ." Duster, *Crusade for Justice*, 169.
p. 66,          "The colored race . . ." McMurry, *To Keep the Waters Troubled*, 210.
p.p. 67-68,     "I thought that it . . ." Duster, *Crusade for Justice*, 219.
p. 68,          "The very frequent . . ." Royster, *Southern Horrors*, 157.
p. 70,          "I was the chief . . ." Duster, *Crusade for Justice*, 232.
p.p. 70-71,     "I felt that I . . ." Ibid., 238.
p. 71,          "So, when at last . . ." Ibid.
p. 71,          "These women did . . ." Ibid., 241.
p. 72,          "I was not too . . ." Ibid., 243.
p. 72,          "When the time . . ." Ibid., 244.

CHAPTER SEVEN: *National Organizations*
p. 74,          "The African Americans in this . . ." McMurry, *To Keep the Waters Troubled*, 245.
p. 75,          "With the birth of . . ." Duster, *Crusade for Justice*, 244.
p. 76,          "To our appeals . . ." McMurry, *To Keep the Waters Troubled*, 258.
p.p. 77-78,     "spent more time . . ." Duster, *Crusade for Justice*, 255.
p. 78,          "pugnacious attitude . . ." Ibid., 255.

p. 78,     "I called attention . . ." Ibid., 255-56.
p. 79,     "President McKinley . . ." McMurry, *To Keep the Waters Troubled*, 253.
p. 81,     "In all things . . ." Ibid., 254.
p. 81,     "Samuel Hose was . . ." Ibid., 255.
p. 82,     "It was a staggering . . ." Duster, *Crusade for Justice*, 258.
p. 82,     "inflict my presence . . ." Ibid., 259.
p. 84,     "The work of that . . ." McMurry, *To Keep the Waters Troubled*, 257.

## CHAPTER EIGHT: *Challenging Authority*
p. 86,     "that he did not . . ." Duster, *Crusade for Justice*, 275.
p. 86,     "My reply to . . ." Ibid., 275-76.
p. 86,     "Miss Addams, there . . ." Ibid., 276.
p. 87,     "taken a leaf . . ." Ibid., 264.
p. 88,     "Mr. Washington's . . ." Ibid., 265.
p. 90,     "All of what she said . . ." Giddings, *Ida: A Sword Among Lions*, 454.
p. 91,     "Mrs. Plummer, the . . ." Duster, *Crusade for Justice*, 283-84.
p. 93,     "Her reply showed . . ." Ibid., 285.
p. 93,     "loss of the . . ." Ibid., 287.
p. 94,     "I did a foolish . . ." Ibid., 325-26.
p.p. 94-95, "the governor to remove . . ." Giddings, *Ida: A Sword Among Lions*, 483.
p. 96,     "for once I . . ." Duster, *Crusade for Justice*, 311.
p. 96,     "I was awakened . . ." Ibid.
p. 96,     "They were intensely . . ." Ibid., 312.

## CHAPTER NINE: *Making a Difference in Illinois*
p. 98,     "to the few . . ." Duster, *Crusade for Justice*, 316.
p. 98,     "Not until that . . ." Ibid.
p.p. 98-99, "Governor, the . . ." Ibid., 317.
p. 99,     "We have done . . ." Ibid., 319.
p. 99,     "If only we had . . ." McMurry, *To Keep the Waters Troubled*, 284.
p. 99,     "that the committee . . ." Duster, *Crusade for Justice*, 326.
p. 101,    "I went home . . ." Ibid., 329.
p. 102,    "Great White Way . . ." Ibid., 300.
p. 102,    "All other races . . ." Ibid., 302.
p. 104,    "The southern women . . ." McMurry, *To Keep the Waters Troubled*, 305.

## CHAPTER TEN: *Final Crusades*
p. 111,    "I would consider . . ." Duster, *Crusade for Justice*, 370.
p. 113,    "good riddance . . ." Ibid., 408.
p. 113,    "I walked down . . ." Ibid.
p. 114,    "Quit talking about . . ." Ibid., 403.
p. 116,    "Although I had . . ." Ibid., 413.
p. 116,    "It took me a . . ." Ibid., 414.
p. 117,    "Because our youth . . ." Ibid., 5.
p. 118,    "no fanfare of . . ." McMurry, *To Keep the Waters Troubled*, 337.

# BIBLIOGRAPHY

Aptheker, Herbert, ed. *A Documentary History of The Negro People in the United States*, 7 vols. New York: The Citadel Press, 1966.

Brundage, W. Fitzhugh, ed. *Under Sentence of Death: Lynching in the South*. Chapel Hill & London: The University of North Carolina Press, 1997.

Campbell, Karlyn Kohrs. *Man Cannot Speak for Her*. 2 vols. New York: Praeger, 1989.

Cartwright, Joseph H. *The Triumph of Jim Crow: Tennessee Race Relations in the 1880s*. Knoxville: The University of Tennessee Press, 1976.

Decosta-Willis, Miriam, ed. *The Memphis Diary of Ida B. Wells*. Boston: Beacon Press, 1995.

Duster, Alfreda M. *Crusade for Justice: The Autobiography of Ida B. Wells*. Chicago and London: The University of Chicago Press, 1970.

Foner, Philip S. *Frederick Douglass*. New York: The Citadel Press, 1950.

————. *Reconstruction: America's Unfinished Revolution*, 1863-1877. New York: Harper & Row Publishers, 1988.

Franklin, John Hope. *From Slavery to Freedom; A History of American Negroes*. New York: Alfred A. Knopf, 1952.

Franklin, John Hope, and August Meier, eds. *Black Leaders of the Twentieth Century*. Urbana: University of Illinois Press, 1982.

Frazier, E. Franklin. *Black Bourgeoisie: The Rise of a New Middle Class*. New York: The Free Press, 1957.

Giddings, Paula. *When and Where I Enter: The Impact of Black Women on Race and Sex in America*. New York: William Morrow and Company, 1984.

————. *Ida: A Sword Among Lions*. New York: HarperCollins Publishers, 2008.

Grant, Donald L. *The Anti-Lynching Movement: 1883-1932*. San Francisco: R and E Research Associates, 1975.

Kellogg, Charles Flint. *NAACP: A History of the National Association for the Advancement of Colored People*. Baltimore: The Johns Hopkins Press, 1967.

Lerner, Gerda, ed. *Black Women in White America: A Documentary History*. New York: Random House, 1972.

Logan, Shirley Wilson, ed. *With Pen and Voice: A Critical Anthology of Nineteenth-Century African-American Women*. Carbondale and Edwardsville: Southern Illinois University Press, 1995.

McMurry, Linda O. *To Keep the Waters Troubled: The Life of Ida B. Wells*. New York: Oxford University Press, 1998.

McPherson, James M. *Ordeal by Fire: The Civil War and Reconstruction*. New York: Alfred A. Knopf, 1982.

Meier, August. *Negro Thought in America, 1880-1915: Racial Ideologies in the Age of Booker T. Washingto*n. Ann Arbor: The University of Michigan Press, 1964.

Mitchell, J. Paul, ed. *Race Riots in Black and White*. Englewood Cliffs, N.J.: Prentice-Hall, Inc. 1970.

Peirce, Paul Skeels. *The Freedman's Bureau: A Chapter in the History of Reconstruction*. New York: Haskell House Publishers, 1971.

Penn, I. Garland. *The Afro-American Press and Its Editors*. New York: Arno Press and The New York Times, 1969.

Pfeifer, Michael J. *Rough Justice: Lynching and American Society, 1874-1947*. Urbana and Chicago: University of Illinois Press, 2004.

Royster, Jacqueline Jones, ed. *Southern Horrors and Other Writings: The Anti-Lynching Campaign of Ida B. Wells, 1892-1900*. Boston & New York: Bedford/St. Martin's, 1997.

Schechter, Patricia A. *Ida B. Wells-Barnett and American Reform, 1880-1930*. Chapel Hill and London: The University of North Carolina Press, 2001.

Schlereth, Thomas J. *Victorian America: Transformations in Everyday Life, 1876-1915*. New York: HarperCollins Publishers, 1991.

Shapiro, Herbert. *White Violence and Black Response: From Reconstruction to Montgomery*. Amherst: The University of Massachusetts Press, 1988.

Spear, Allan. *Black Chicago: The Making of a Negro Ghetto, 1890-1920*. Chicago: The University of Chicago Press, 1967.

Sterling, Dorothy. *Black Foremothers: Three Lives*. New York: The Feminist Press at the City University of New York, 1988.

Thompson, Mildred I. *Ida B. Wells-Barnett: An Exploratory Study of an American Black Woman*, 1893-1930. Brooklyn: Carlson Publishing, 1990.

Thornbrough, Emma Lou. *T. Thomas Fortune: Militant Journalist*. Chicago and London: University of Chicago Press, 1972.

Tuttle, William Jr. *Race Riot: Chicago in the Red Summer of 1919*. New York: Atheneum, 1978.

Woodward, C. Vann. *The Strange Career of Jim Crow*. New York: Oxford University Press, 1974.

# WEB SITES

http://www.idabwells.org

Created and maintained by the Ida B. Wells-Barnett family, this site features a brief biography, a timeline of Ida's life, and information about the Spires Bolling House in Holly Springs, Mississippi, which is the site of the Ida B. Wells Museum.

http://www.gutenberg.org/browse/authors/w#a5765

Works by Ida B. Wells-Barnett are available for download on this Project Gutenberg site.

http://www.nps.gov/history/nr/travel/civilrights/il2.htm

The late-nineteenth-century Romanesque Revival style house in which Ida B. Wells-Barnett lived in Chicago is featured on this Web site. "We Shall Overcome. Historic Places of the Civil Rights Movement" is a project of the U.S. government.

# INDEX

# PICTURE CREDITS

6:       R. Gates/Hulton Archive/Getty Images

8:       Courtesy of Library of Congress

13:      Courtesy of Library of Congress

15:      Courtesy of Library of Congress

19:      Kevin Britland / Alamy

20-21:  Courtesy of Library of Congress

23:      Courtesy of Library of Congress

25:      Courtesy of Library of Congress

27:      World History Archive/Alamy

37:      Courtesy of Library of Congress

38:      Background: Used under license from iStockphoto

42-43:  Courtesy of Library of Congress

47:      Special Collections research Center, University of Chicago Library

54:      Courtesy of Library of Congress

60:      Courtesy of Library of Congress

62:      Courtesy of Library of Congress

65:      Courtesy of Library of Congress

66:      Courtesy of Library of Congress

69:      Courtesy of Library of Congress

70:      Courtesy of Library of Congress

74:      Courtesy of Library of Congress

77:      Courtesy of Library of Congress

78:      Courtesy of Library of Congress

80:      Courtesy of Library of Congress

83:      Courtesy of University of Illinois at Chicago, University Library, Jane Addams Memorial Collection

87:      Courtesy of Library of Congress

88:      Courtesy of Library of Congress

92:      Courtesy of Special Collections and Archives, W. E. B. Du Bois Library, University of Massachusetts, Amherst

100:     Courtesy of Library of Congress

105:     Courtesy of Library of Congress

108:     Courtesy of Library of Congress

110:     Courtesy of University of Illinois at Chicago, University Library, Jane Addams Memorial Collection

113:     Courtesy of Library of Congress

118:     Courtesy of University of Illinois at Chicago, University Library, Jane Addams Memorial Collection

**DATE DUE**

OC 2 4 '11